THE ALHAMBRA

D0609040

Robert Irwin lives in London. His fiction includes *The Arabian Nightmare* (1983) and *Exquisite Corpse* (1995). His many books and articles on Islamic subjects include *The Arabian Nights: A Companion* (1994), *Islamic Art* (1997) and *Night & Horses & the Desert: An Anthology of Classical Arabic Literature*. He is a Fellow of the Royal Society of Literature and a Fellow of the London Institute of Pataphysics.

ALSO BY ROBERT IRWIN

The Middle East in the Middle Ages:
the Early Mameluke Sultanate 1250–1382

The Arabian Nights: a Companion

Islamic Art

Night and Horses and the Desert:
an Anthology of Classical Arabic Literature

Also six novels, the most recent of which is
Satan Wants Me

THE ALHAMBRA

ROBERT IRWIN

P

PROFILE BOOKS

This paperback edition published in 2005

First published in Great Britain in 2004 by
Profile Books Ltd
58A Hatton Garden
London ECIN 8LX
www.profilebooks.co.uk

Copyright © Robert Irwin, 2004, 2005

1 3 5 7 9 10 8 6 4 2

Typeset in Caslon by MacGuru Ltd
info@macguru.org.uk
Designed by Peter Campbell
Printed and bound in Great Britain by
Bookmarque Ltd, Croydon, Surrey

A CIP catalogue record for this book is available from the
British Library.

ISBN 1 86197 487 6

CONTENTS

CHRONOLOGY

711	Arabs enter Spain.
755	'Abd al-Rahman I establishes Umayyad emirate in Spain.
c.*880s*	The first version of the Alcazaba, or citadel of the Alhambra, built.
928	The Umayyad 'Abd al-Rahman III takes the title of Caliph.
936	Foundation of the Umayyad Palace of Madinat al-Zahra outside Cordova.
1013	Sack of Umayyad Cordova.
1031	End of the Umayyad dynasty and beginning of the age of *Ta'ifa* or Petty Kings.
1085	Fall of Muslim Toledo to Christian Castile.
1230	Ibn al-Ahmar establishes Nasrid rule over Granada and becomes the last Muslim ruler in Spain.
c.*1320s*	Building of the first version of the Mexuar.
1333–54	Reign of Nasrid Yusuf I over Granada. During his reign the Comares Palace is built.
1354–9	First reign of Muhammad V (followed by exile in Morocco).
1362–91	Second reign of Muhammad V. Additions to the Comares Palace and the building of the Court of the Lions.

INTRODUCTION

The Alhambra is Spain's best-kept secret. This glorious medieval palace, which resembles a child's toy castle, sits on the Assabica hills. (Assabica is Arabic for red.) The palace was built in the years 1334–91 and was the seat of the magnificent Nasrid caliphs. What stories this building could tell if only it could speak! Despite the austerity of the palace's outward appearance, its immaculately restored interior more closely resembles a lady's boudoir. However, there are no statues or figurative paintings in the palace, as Islam strictly forbids images of any kind. Like Hittite and Ottoman palaces, the palace of the Alhambra was divided into three sections. First, there was the Mexuar, the chamber where public business was transacted. Members of the public could penetrate no further into the palace than the Mexuar. At the end of the Mexuar is a small private chapel that was built by the Catholic monarchs, Ferdinand and Isabella, after they conquered the palace in 1492. Beyond the Mexuar, there was the Court of the Myrtles where more private administrative business was conducted and where ambassadors were received. (It was in the Hall of the Ambassadors that Columbus presented his scheme to cross the Atlantic to the Catholic monarchs of Aragon and Castile.) The goldfish pool is the central pivot of the Court of the Myrtles.

Finally, the private apartments of the king and his wives and concubines were located in the Court of the Lions. Off the Court of the Lions, one enters the Hall of the Two Sisters, which was the private apartment of the king's favourite concubine of the moment. (Note its trompe-l'oeil ceiling.) The Lindaraxa chamber that leads off it was the dressing room of the favourite. Then there is the Gossip Room, which was a factory of intrigue. Finally, do not miss the Hall of the Kings and its celebrated dancing room. This was also the place where great roistering feasts were held. Though the Court of the Lions was home to the royal harem, its eunuch guards did not guard it carefully enough. In the Hall of the Abencerrages (and here note another trompe-l'oeil ceiling based on a theorem by Pythagoras), the Sultan Boabdil, having invited thirty-nine members of the Abencerrage clan to dinner, had them all slaughtered, after he had discovered that one of them had been having an affair with his favourite concubine, Zorayda. The struggle for the affections of Zorayda led directly to the fall of Granada to the Christians in 1492. The paintings on the ceiling of the nearby Hall of the Kings were done by a Spanish Christian painter and depict historical scenes. The Lion Fountain, that gives this part of the palace its name, was originally made for a Jewish palace of the eleventh century, but subsequently it had its Jewish imagery erased and Muslim motifs were substituted. The twelve lions, that support the fountain and leer at the tourists, symbolise the twelve signs of the zodiac and the four water channels that cross the courtyard represent the four rivers of paradise. After 1492 the palace fell into dilapidation, but during the Peninsular War, the Duke of Wellington chased out the chickens, beggars and gypsies and made his home in the Alhambra. He also planted elm trees all the way down the slopes of the Alhambra hill. Conclude your tour by visiting the Generalife (Arabic for Garden of the Architect), which was the Nasrid

Emirs' summer palace to which they would flee to escape the pomp and protocol of the palace. It was in the neighbouring Garden of the Sultana that the lustrously beautiful Zorayda met her trysting Abencerrage lover. The timeless beauty of the palace and its gardens offers us an unparalleled window into the Moorish past.

⧗

Not one 'fact' in the preceding two paragraphs is likely to be correct. Yet I have carefully compiled it from material drawn from real and current guidebooks. Their misinformation has the advantage of being clear and colourful. Richard Ford, author of *A Handbook for Travellers in Spain* (1845) defended the legends made for tourists and declared that the Alhambra was situated beyond the jurisdiction of sober history, for 'where fairies have danced their mystic rings, flowers may spring, but mere grass will never grow'. Hmm. The real history of the Alhambra is sadly much less clear, owes little to fairies, and Zorayda has no place in it whatsoever. What follows in this Introduction is a brief rundown of the essentials, though, as will be apparent in the ensuing chapters, there are very few facts about the Alhambra that are securely established and agreed upon. It is a sunlit place of many mysteries.

The finest example of a medieval Muslim palace is in Western Europe. Indeed, the Alhambra is the only Muslim palace to survive from the Middle Ages. It is superbly sited, looking down on Granada, one of the chief cities of the Spanish region of Andalusia. Modern Andalusia (or, in Spanish, Andalucia) consists of eight provinces located in the southernmost part of the Iberian Peninsula: Malaga, Cadiz,

Seville, Huelva, Cordoba, Jaen, Almeria and Granada. Although Andalusia nowadays refers only to the southern-most region of Spain, in the Middle Ages Andalusia (or, in Arabic, al-Andalus) referred to that part of the Iberian Peninsula that was under Muslim control, which was most of it. In 711 Arab and Berber armies crossed the Straits of Gibraltar and swiftly occupied all but the north-west corner of the peninsula. Muslim armies also briefly occupied the South of France and some troops even ventured into what is now Switzerland. (A few decades ago the frozen bodies of an Arab raider and his camel were discovered under Swiss snow.) 'Moor' is a term often used to describe the Arab and Berber inhabitants of Spain and North Africa (from the Latin, *Maurus*, an inhabitant of the North African region of Mauretania). It is also sometimes used more vaguely to describe a black man or one with a swarthy complexion, as, for example, Othello, 'the Moor of Venice'. Muslims retained a substantial grip on Spain until 1492, when their last remaining territory in the region of Granada was conquered by the Christians. However, for most of the Middle Ages a substantial part of Europe had been under Muslim control. (Sicily was for a long time another Muslim province.) Muslim science, art and literature, as developed in the courts of Cordoba, Seville, Granada and Palermo, are all part of Europe's cultural heritage.

In the late seventh and early eighth centuries most of the Muslim world was governed by an Arab dynasty of caliphs known as the Umayyads, who claimed to rule as successors of the Prophet Muhammad. In 750 they were overthrown by a rival clan known as the Abbasids. From 750 until 1258 the Abbasid caliphs either ruled or at least pretended to rule over the Muslim heartlands of the Middle East. The Abbasid capital in Baghdad was also for centuries Islam's chief centre of culture. However, 'Abd al-Rahman, a member of the defeated Umayyad clan, succeeded in escaping the Abbasid purge of the Umayyads and their supporters. He fled to Spain and from 755 onwards 'Abd al-Rahman and his Umayyad successors ruled there. The Umayyad caliphate in Spain fell apart in the early decades of the eleventh century and various smaller Muslim principalities were carved out of its ruins. One by one, though, they fell to the Christian *Reconquista*. Granada was the last principality to survive, but in 1492 Granada and the Alhambra were surrendered to Ferdinand and Isabella, the monarchs of Castile and Aragon. Thereafter, the Alhambra became a Christian palace for a while, before being allowed to go to rack and ruin. Its restoration followed its 'discovery' by romantic travellers and writers in the nineteenth century.

The Alhambra, situated on a rocky spur on the northern edge of the city of Granada, is not one palace, but several palaces and supporting buildings put up over a long time. There was a citadel on the western tip of the Sabika hill as early as the ninth century. On the other hand, parts of the Alhambra were erected as late as the mid-fifteenth century. However, the most substantial and most interesting parts were built in the mid- to late-fourteenth century. The Cuarto Dorado, Court of Myrtles and Court of the Lions all date from this period. The Partal was erected at the beginning of that century. The Mexuar has undergone so many changes over the centuries that it cannot sensibly be said to date from any period. The Alhambra was the residence and seat of government of the Nasrids, an Arab dynasty, whose founder

1. Viewed from the outside, the Alhambra looks military and austere.

usurped power in Granada around 1238. The layout of the various parts of the Alhambra is decidedly difficult to grasp, as rooms, courtyards and passageways are set at odd angles to one another. There is no grand overarching design. Though the extravagance and intricacy of the palaces' decoration is overwhelming, the scale of the buildings is intimate.

The naming of parts is basic to the understanding of the Alhambra, but different guidebooks refer to the same places by different names. Most of the names are fanciful and seem to have been coined in the post-medieval period. The palatial buildings in the main cluster are now interconnected (see pages 12–13), though this was not the case in the Middle Ages. This group of buildings is known in Spanish as the Palacio de los Nazaríes (the Nasrid Palace), or the Casa Real (the Royal House). All books refer to the Mexuar, at the western end of this palace complex, as the Mexuar. The name is supposed to be a Spanish deformation of the Arabic *mashawar*, meaning place of counsel, and this seems entirely plausible, though I cannot find the precise Arabic word in my dictionaries. I did find *mashawir*, which means 'an instrument for collecting honey', *mishwar* meaning 'a horse-show' and *mashawara*, meaning 'to walk to and fro'. (By the way, the 'x' in Spanish names such as Mexuar and Lindaraxa is pronounced as a 'sh'. A high proportion of Spanish words with an 'x' in them derive from Arabic, the 'x' replacing the Arabic letter, *shin*.) The next place one comes to on the tourist itinerary is the Cuarto Dorado. Cuarto Dorado is Spanish for 'Golden Room' and, here again, all the guidebooks seem to be agreed in calling this area the Cuarto Dorado. The case is more complicated with the adjoining architectural complex, which is designated as the Court of the Myrtles, or, in Spanish, Patio de los Arrayanes, because of the myrtle bushes that line the long central pool in the middle of the courtyard. But this group of rooms round the courtyard with the myrtles is also known as the Comares Palace, or Palacio de Comares (though there is no agreement whatsoever as to why it is so called). As we shall see, it is most unlikely that the medieval Arabs who built and inhabited this place referred to it by either of these names. The Sala de la Barca on the north side of the Court of the Myrtles either gets its name from the Spanish for 'boat' or the Arabic for 'blessing' (see Chapter 1 on this). Whatever the meaning of the name, it seems to be one that has been handed down for centuries and perhaps it was what Muslims called it. The same may apply to the Hall of the Ambassadors, or Salón de Embajadores, to which the Sala de la Barca serves as an antechamber. Although almost everyone refers to this large room as the Hall of the

Ambassadors, the leading Spanish expert on the Alhambra, Antonio Fernández-Puertas, calls this the Salón de Comares. The Sala de la Barca and the Hall of the Ambassadors are both within what is known as the Comares Tower.

Continuing with the tourist route, one next comes to the Sala de los Mocárabes, which takes its name from the ornate stalactitic decoration of its ceiling, but that ceiling no longer exists, as it was destroyed in a fire centuries ago. I am reminded of a dialogue the anthropologist Nigel Barley had with an African Dowayo tribesman. He wanted to know who had organised a particular festival. The reply came: 'The man with the porcupine quills in his hair.'

'I can't see anyone with porcupine quills in his hair,' Barley said.

'No, he's not wearing them.'

Some books also refer to Sala de los Mocárabes as the Harem. That is their fantasy. This chamber is on the west side of the Court of the Lions (or Patio de los Leones), so called because of the lions that seem to support the fountain at its centre. On the east side is the Hall of the Kings (in Spanish, Sala de los Reyes), so called because some have identified the paintings in that hall as portraits of Nasrid rulers of Granada. On the north side of the Court of the Lions is what is usually known as the Hall of the Two Sisters (in Spanish, Sala de las Dos Hermanas). However, Fernández-Puertas calls this room the Qubba Major (a yoking of Arabic and Spanish, meaning the 'Great Domed Chamber'). A smaller room leads out from it to the north, known as the Sala de los Ajimeces (probably deriving from the Arabic *shimasas*, referring to a lattice screen against the sun), and this in turn leads on to the Mirador de la Daraxa. A *mirador* is a belvedere, or viewing point. Daraxa has been interpreted with varying degrees of confidence as the 'House' or 'Palace of Aisha'. Lindaraxa, an alternative label for this belvedere, can be read as a Spanish deformation of the Arabic *'Ayn dar Aisha*, or 'eye of the house of 'Aisha'. The Hall of the Abencerrages, or, in Spanish, Abencerrajes, is situated on the south side of the Court of the Lions. Various spellings of Abencerrages are permissible, though the word is a loose European rendering of the Arabic *Banu Sarraj* (literally 'the Sons of the Saddlemaker'). The entirely fanciful name for the room is derived, I think, from a nineteenth-century novel by Chateaubriand. The essential truth about the main group of buildings within the Alhambra is that it consists of two sets of apartments, the one centred round the Court of the Myrtles and the other round the Court of the Lions, but we do not know for sure what either set of apartments was called by the medieval Arabs who used to inhabit them. We will return to this question.

The Alcazaba to the west of the Nasrid Palace was the citadel and it takes its name from the Arabic *al-qasaba*, meaning 'the citadel'. ('Al' means 'the' in Arabic.) Its principal tower is the Torre de la Vela (the Watch Tower). The sixteenth-century Palace of Charles V is to the south of the Muslim palace complex. What is left of the Partal Palace is to the east of the main palace complex, but I have not been able to discover why it is so called. The name does not sound Arab. (Indeed, there is no 'p' in the Arabic alphabet.) According to one usually reliable guidebook I consulted, an open portico is known as 'a partal in Arabic', but none of my Arabic dictionaries confirmed this. The closest I got to

2. Over the centuries the Alhambra has suffered from fires, an explosion in a
gunpowder store, selective demolition, neglect and tourists. In the nineteenth
century it was common for visitors to carve their names on the walls and to
take tiles and chippings of stone and stucco away with them. (Some of this
tourist loot has ended up in the British Museum and the Victoria and Albert
Museum.) This illustration by Gustav Doré appeared in Baron Charles
Davillier's *L'Espagne* (1874). Davillier actually witnessed this scene during his
tour of the country.

'partal' in Arabic was the cluster of words associated with the root verb *bartala*, having to do with bribery, though, according to Edward William Lane's *English–Arabic Lexicon*, the verb *bartala* also means 'to place a long stone in the fore part of a watering trough'. However, Fernández-Puertas believes that *bartal* is indeed an Arabic corruption of the Latin *porticus*. The portico of the Partal is known as the Torre de las Damas (Tower of the Ladies). It is not known why.

The two paragraphs with which this Introduction opened are dispiriting to contemplate. But legends, lies and honest mistakes are as much a part of the story of the Alhambra as is the factual record. So are vandalism, inadequately researched and botched restoration work and distortions caused by the demands of the tourist trade. In the first chapter, I will discuss the layout of the Alhambra in some detail, focusing always on the fact that what you see is not what the medieval Arab saw. The second chapter covers the social and political background behind the building of the Alhambra and questions whether one of its supposed palaces is really a palace at all. The third chapter explores the respective contributions of the artisan, the mathematician and the philosopher to the design and construction of the palaces. The fourth and final chapter deals with the afterlife of the Alhambra in Western and Arab literature as well as in architecture, painting and music.

THE PALACES OF THE ALHAMBRA

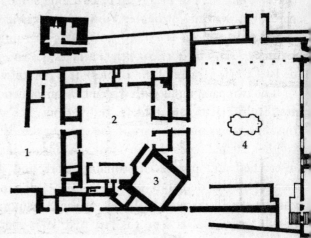

Public en

1. Small entrance square
2. First court
3. Ruins of mosque
4. Court of Machuca
5. Oratory
6. Mexuar
7. Court of the Cuarto Dorado
8. Cuarto Dorado
9. Court of the Myrtles
10. Sala de la Barca
11. Hall of the Ambassadors

12. Bath
13. Tower of the Peinador de la Reina
14. Garden
15. Court of the Lions
16. Sala de los Mocárabes
17. Hall of the Kings
18. Hall of the Two Sisters
19. Mirador of Lindaraxa
20. Hall of the Abencerrages
21. *Rawdah*
22. Chapel of the Palace of Charles V

Source: Oleg Grabar, *The Alhambra*, 1978

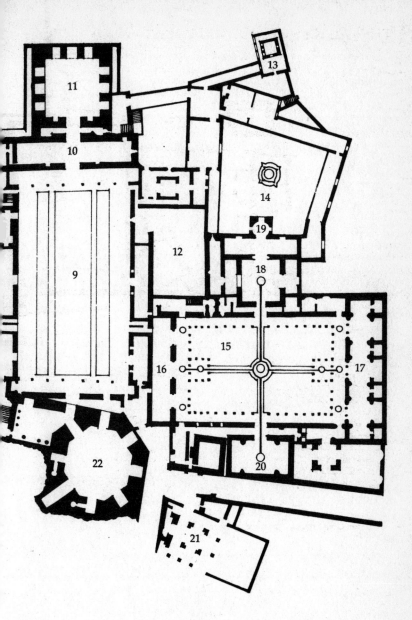

I

·····························

THE FAIRY-TALE PALACE?

I have heard O King, that the king walked to the center of the palace and looked around, but saw no one. The palace was furnished with silk carpets and leather mats and hung with drapes. There were also settees, benches, and seats with cushions, as well as cupboards. In the middle there stood a spacious courtyard, surrounded by four adjoining recessed courts facing each other. In the center stood a fountain, on top of which crouched four lions in red gold, spouting water from their mouths in droplets that looked like gems and pearls, and about the fountain singing birds fluttered under a high net to prevent them flying away ...

'The Tale of the King's Son and the She-Ghoul', *The Arabian Nights*, translated by Hussein Haddawy (New York and London, 1990)

Many who have visited the buildings of the Alhambra judge them to be the most beautiful in the world. The ingenious design of the palaces and the richness of the ornamentation offer the eye easy pleasures. The Alhambra looks like a Hollywood version of an oriental palace – and, indeed, both the Court of the Myrtles and the Court of the Lions have been used as sets in Ray Harryhausen's Sinbad films. Though the Alhambra is easy to enjoy, it is much harder to understand. The more closely one studies the functions and the iconography of its various parts and tries to establish how the place was inhabited, the more mysterious the buildings and their inhabitants seem. There are limits to what the historian and archaeologist can retrieve.

The history of medieval Spain is, more than anything else, the struggle for supremacy in that peninsula between the Muslims and Christians. For centuries after the Arab and Berber invasion in the early eighth century, almost all of Spain and Portugal lay under Muslim rule. The Christian *Reconquista* of Spain began to get under way only in the mid-eleventh century. (It was a precursor of the Crusades against the Muslims in the East that started at the end of that same century.) One by one the great Muslim centres in Spain – Toledo, Cordoba and Seville among them – fell to Christian armies. The attack on Granada at the end of the fifteenth century was the final offensive in a centuries' old struggle between the armies of Christendom and Islam. In January 1492 the Muslim kingdom of Granada, the last Islamic foothold in Spain, surrendered to the armies of the Catholic monarchs Ferdinand and Isabella. The last sultan of Granada, Abu Abdallah Muhammad XII, known in the West as Boabdil, sighed his legendary last sigh before taking ship to North Africa and exile in Tlemcen. (Much later, Charles V, on first entering the Alhambra, commented, 'Ill-fated was the man who lost all this!')

Columbus was among those who witnessed the surrender of Granada, and 1492 was also the year that he set sail across the Atlantic in the quest for a new route to the Indies. Among the people who accompanied him on the voyage of discovery was Luis de Torres, an Arabic-speaking Jew. De Torres was supposed to act as interpreter when they reached the spice and silk markets of the Indies, for in the late fifteenth century Arabic- and Persian-speaking Muslims dominated maritime commerce in Asian waters. Therefore, when Columbus touched land at what was in fact Cuba, but which he believed to be Japan, Luis de Torres was there beside him to address the mystified Taínos natives in Arabic. Like Ferdinand and Isabella's onslaught against the last remaining Muslim strongholds in Spain, Columbus's mission was seen by him and his royal patrons as part of a global Crusade against Islam. He hoped that in crossing the Atlantic, he would be able to make direct contact with the Mongol Great Khan, to allow missionaries to preach the Christian faith in India and to secure access to the spices of the Far East without having to deal with Mameluke or Ottoman intermediaries.

> Your highnesses, as good Christian and Catholic princes, devout and propagators of the Christian faith, as well as enemies of the sect of Mahomet and of idolatries and heresies, conceived the plan of sending me, Christopher Columbus, to this country of the Indies, there to see the princes, the peoples, the territory, their disposition and all things else, and the way in which one might proceed to convert these regions to our holy faith.

So the *Journal* ascribed to Columbus described his mission. For the rest of his life Columbus continued to be obsessed with plans to retake Jerusalem and in so doing fulfil holy prophecies. However, though the conquest of Granada was a belated triumph of the crusading movement, the great age of crusading was over and Spanish attempts in the sixteenth century to establish themselves in North

Africa were only intermittently successful. The Alhambra survived better than the rest of Hispano-Arabic culture. When Ferdinand and Isabella took possession of Granada, they promised to tolerate the Muslim faith, but, within a decade Cardinal Ximenes had persuaded Isabella to issue a decree that offered the Muslims the choice between conversion and exile. Mosques were closed and there were vast bonfires of Arabic manuscripts. When later, in the 1560s, Philip II sought to enforce a ban on the Arab language, costume and customs, the Moors of the Alpuxarras highlands rebelled. By 1570 the rebels had been subdued and killed, enslaved or sent into exile. The nineteenth-century Protestant English historian Stanley Lane-Poole wrote of the aftermath of their defeat in the following terms:

> The true memorial of the Moors is seen in the desolate tracts of utter barrenness, where once the Moslem grew luxuriant vines and olives and yellow ears of corn; in a stupid, ignorant population where once wit and learning flourished; in the general stagnation and degradation of a people which has hopelessly fallen in the scale of nations, and deserved its humiliation.

In part, the Alhambra survived under Christian rule because it was regarded as a victory monument of the *Reconquista*. But it seems also to have been the case that Ferdinand and Isabella were enchanted by the beauty of the place they moved into. They were also quite familiar with the Moorish way of life and sometimes chose to wear Arab dress. Not only did the Alhambra survive under the administration of the Catholic monarchs, it is the only medieval Islamic palace of which a substantial part has survived to the present day (even though less has survived than would first appear). Almost every Abbasid caliph in eighth- and ninth-century Baghdad built his own palace and let his predecessor's fall into ruin. Some of these palaces were on a vast scale, but no trace of them remains and we know of them only from literary sources. From 836 to 892 Samarra was the Abbasid capital and a succession of palaces was built along a forty-kilometre stretch of the Tigris, but only aerial photography coupled with careful archaeology has established the bare outlines of their foundations. Low-level ruins remain of the Ghaznavid palace of Ghazna in Afghanistan. Though the Topkapi Palace of the Ottoman sultans in Istanbul was founded in the late fifteenth century, most of what survives today was put up in later centuries.

In Spain itself the foundations of Madinat al-Zahra, the tenth-century Umayyad palace outside Cordoba, are easily visible and some of the walls are still standing (and such is the progress of archaeology that more walls seem to be still standing each time one visits the place). However, though attempts have been made to establish some sort of genealogical link between the Alhambra and the Madinat al-Zahra, the two foundations do not have much in common. In the first place, the Madinat al-Zahra, built at a time when the Umayyad caliphate in Spain was at the peak of its splendour, was a much more lavish building, which made extravagant use of marble and bronze, as well as silver and gold mosaics. The walls and ceiling of the caliph's reception hall were lit up by reflected flashes of light from a great pool of mercury. In comparison, the Alhambra's 'splendour' was acquired on the cheap.

Secondly, the Madinat al-Zahra was a single carefully

3. An aerial view of the tenth-century palace of Madinat al-Zahra, the residence of the Umayyad Caliphs of Cordoba, five kilometres outside that city. The palace extends down a hillside and the caliph's own rooms and the ceremonial chambers were at the top of the hill and commanded a view of the rest of the palace complex. The caliph's ministers were accommodated at a lower level and servants and garrison at a lower level yet. Unlike the later palaces of the Alhambra, the Madinat al-Zahra is a single compact rectangle. Again, unlike the Alhambra, the Umayyad palace relied on soldiers rather than fortifications to defend it.

designed and integrated unit (like such Western palaces as Versailles or Buckingham Palace), whereas the Alhambra is really a palace-city and has more in common with such sprawling complexes as Samarra, where there were not only several palaces, but also barracks, mosques, administrative buildings, racecourses and a game reserve. Some modern scholars have tried to present the Alhambra as a typical Islamic palace, but it is questionable whether there was any such thing. In some ways it resembled the Forbidden City in Beijing more closely than it did earlier Muslim palaces in Spain

The walls of the Alhambra complex enclosed not one but perhaps as many as six palaces, a barracks, a congregational mosque and a small town, as well as a zoo, an aviary and industrial workshops. The palace-city had its own *qadi*, or judge, and most of the shops and services that could be found in the city of Granada could also be found in the Alhambra which overlooked it. The whole site occupies fourteen hectares and it has been estimated that it could accommodate 40,000 people. Therefore the Arab sources referred to the area not as a *qasr* (palace), but as a *madina* (town), for the place was a city in its own right.

The Alhambra derives its name from the Arabic for 'the red', *al-hamra*. Presumably this refers to the red ferruginous dust that has stained the stone walls of the citadel. It is situated on a spur of rock of the Sierra Nevada. Ibn Battuta, who visited Granada in the early fourteenth century, described the countryside as follows: 'It is surrounded on all sides by orchards, gardens, meadows, palaces and vineyards'. Under the dynasty of Nasrid sultans, who ruled Granada from 1232 until 1492, the Sierra Nevada was designated as a royal *hayr* or closed hunting park. The Nasrid rulers probably spent most of their life out of doors and the palaces of the Alhambra can be seen as a cluster of rural villas, serving as a base for hunting expeditions, picnics and tours of inspection of farms and flocks. One consequence of this was that the Alhambra was mostly inhabited by the princes and courtiers at night and the place seems to have been designed with this in mind. After the composer Manuel de Falla had taken the British musicologist and Hispanist J. B. Trend round the Alhambra late one night in 1919 to show off what Falla considered the place's operatic qualities, Trend was driven to remark that 'Most architecture is intended for the daytime ... The Alhambra was built to be seen at night; it was carefully planned, I think, for that and nothing else. Parts of it which seem almost meaningless in sunshine seem to "come off" completely at night.' And Washington Irving wrote more floridly in *The Alhambra* about the effects of moonlight: 'Every rent and chasm of time, every mouldering tint and weather-stain disappears, the marble resumes its original whiteness, the long colonnades brighten in the moon beams, the halls are illuminated with a softened radiance, until the whole edifice reminds one of the enchanted palace of an Arabian tale.'

The *qasida* (ode) by the fourteenth-century poet and vizier Ibn Zamrak that is inscribed on the dado of the Hall of the Two Sisters, and which celebrates the hall's manifold glories, issues the following boast:

And how many arches rise up in its vault supported by
columns which at night are embellished by light!
You would think that they are the heavenly spheres whose

[22]

orbits revolve, overshadowing the pillar of dawn when it
barely begins to appear after having passed through the
night.

Surviving accounts suggest that medieval Muslim princes spent huge sums on vast candles – a speciality of medieval Damascus. The palaces of the Alhambra all seem to have been lit from below. Ibn al-Khatib, the Nasrid vizier and court poet, writing about the 1362 festivities to mark the Prophet's birthday, remarked on the 'standing candelabras of bronze and glass with wide bases, thick stems and many pendant candle-sockets'. Only in the Great Mosque were there lamps suspended from the ceiling.

The rocky spur overlooking the city of Granada was a natural site for a fortress. From the ninth century onwards the western corner of the spur was fortified. The surviving *Qasaba* (Arabic, citadel), or in modern Spanish the Alcazaba, was built on the older foundations by the founder of the Nasrid dynasty, Muhammad I, also known as Ibn al-Ahmar (1232–73). The military compound of the Alcazaba eventually included a parade ground, alleys and subterranean dungeons. He also enclosed the whole spur with a perimeter wall and completed an aqueduct in 1238. Once the supply of water had been assured, the spur was habitable and became the site not just of several palaces and barracks and a mosque, but also of workshops, and the residences of those in royal service. Most of the workshops and humbler residences were in the upper zone to the east of the royal palaces. The area included a tannery, a mint, *hammam*s (public baths), pottery and glass kilns and shops. Three main streets – Calle Real Baja, Calle Real Alta and Calle de Ronda – ran through the artisanal zone.

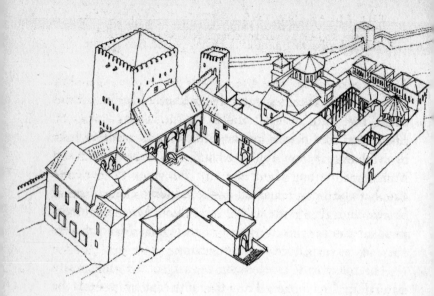

4. This three-dimensional sketch gives a much clearer idea of the awkward way the two main courtyard complexes, those of the Court of the Myrtles and the Court of the Lions, were soldered together. Court of the Myrtles is at the forefront, with Court of the Lions a little behind it to the right. Originally the two complexes were quite separate.

THE ALCAZABA, THE PARTAL, THE MEXUAR,
THE CUARTO DORADO AND THE COURT
OF THE MYRTLES

The Alcazaba is the oldest remaining part of the Alhambra complex. Only some fragmentary foundations survive of the palace that once stood to the east of the main cluster of palaces and the Great Mosque and which was probably built by Muhammad II (1273–1302) and extensively rebuilt by Muhammad V (1354–9 and 1362–91). This seems to have consisted of a great portico and a courtyard with a long channel of water at its centre. However, after 1492 it was demolished to make way for the Convent of San Francisco and that in turn was eventually converted into the state-run Parador Nacional de San Francisco. Similarly, only archaeologically excavated foundations now remain of the late thirteenth- or very early fourteenth-century Palace of the Abencerrages on the southern side of the Alhambra enclosure. This seems to have had a central patio and large pool. The French blew the place up when they occupied the Alhambra during the Peninsular War and much of the remaining ruins were destroyed in 1957 to make a car park.

The oldest partially surviving palace is the Partal Palace built by Muhammad III (1302–9). This is situated to the east of the Court of the Lions and in medieval times was separated from it by crowded streets. The remaining portico of the Partal is known as the Torre de las Damas (Tower of the Ladies) and it may have faced a similar building at the opposite end of the pool, just like the Court of the Myrtles of the Comares Palace, though there does not seem to be any archaeological evidence for this. Most of the gallery's painted decoration has faded away. Originally the gallery of the portico rested on square pillars, but in the twentieth century they were replaced by round columns for no good reason. The archaeologist responsible for this blunder, Leopoldo Torres Balbás (1888–1960), took similarly bold and erroneous decisions concerning the restoration of other areas of the Alhambra, including the Court of the Lions and the gardens of the palaces. Indeed, he deserves to be considered one of the architects of the Alhambra as we have it today. In the late nineteenth century, the Torre de las Damas was sold to a private buyer and converted into a house, which resulted in the destruction of much of the decoration. In due course the Partal was bought by the banker Arturo Gwinner Dreiss. Though he eventually sold back the building to the Spanish government, he kept the ceiling of the tower and this ended up in 1978 in the Museum für Islamische Kunst, in Berlin. (On a much smaller scale, nineteenth-century tourists liked to chip off bits of tile and stucco from the Alhambra and take them home as souvenirs. Murray's *Handbook to Spain* of 1912 has this to say on the subject: 'Too much cannot be said against the vulgar and rather disgusting habit of cutting names and tearing off pieces of plaster and tiles from the Alhambra.' Yet the holdings of institutions such as the British Museum would be poorer without such Victorian tourist clippings.) The box-hedging and the ivy of the Partal's garden are anachronistic, as are all the gardens of the Alhambra in almost all their details, though certainly pleasant to look upon.

The next oldest surviving palace is the Palace of the Court of Myrtles, also known as the Comares Palace. Myrtle bushes line the long pool that is the central feature of this palace. It is not certain where the name Comares comes from.

5. Dating from the early fourteenth century, the Partal Palace consists of a tower, portico and pool. This palace is really a glorified belvedere, commanding views of the mountains to the north and its own garden to the south. Here and elsewhere reflections in water reinforce the impact of the architecture of the Alhambra.

According to some authorities, it derives from *qumariyya*, the Arabic for multicoloured stained glass (of the sort one sees in the Balcony of the Hall of the Ambassadors). However, I cannot find this word in any of my Arabic dictionaries. (The Arabic root form '*qamr*' generates words mostly relating to the moon and to gambling, though *qamar* means 'snow-blindness', *qamar al-din* is a kind of jelly made from apricots, *qumri* is a kind of turtle-dove and *qumra* a greenish-white colour. Perhaps *qumariyya* refers to the place's appearance by moonlight, so often admired by its visitors.) According to one authority on the Alhambra, James Dickie, Qumarish is a North African place name and it refers to the artisans who worked on this building. The uncertainty about the origin of the name Comares is typical. As we shall see, there is uncertainty and dispute about every single feature of the Alhambra – its architecture, chronology, iconography, nomenclature and the way it was originally occupied. We are dealing not so much with a body of knowledge as with a body of wild guesses. For what it is worth, Ibn al-Khatib in the fourteenth century referred to the Comares Palace as the *Qasr* (Palace) of the Sultan. But study of the Alhambra is generally bedevilled by the different names – Spanish, English or Arabic – given to the various parts of the palaces, many of which are in any case quite fanciful.

The building of the Comares Palace was initiated by the Nasrid ruler of Granada, Ismail I (1314–25), and continued by Yusuf I (1333–54), though he was assassinated before he could complete the work. So Muhammad V finished it in 1370. The original courtyard through which one entered the Comares Palace complex has been demolished and only a small part of the second courtyard, the Machuca court, survives. Today it is from the Machuca that one reaches the Mexuar, or council chamber (from the Arabic *mashwar*, a place of council), but this was not the Mexuar's original entrance. This building was first erected by Yusuf I but then mostly demolished and rebuilt by Muhammad V in 1362. A contemporary poem by Ibn al-Khatib describes how a party was held, ostensibly in honour of the Prophet's birthday but in effect to show off the new building.

The Mexuar resembles the axe of George Washington, which is legendarily preserved in some American museum. Although the wooden haft rotted and was replaced and subsequently the iron axe-head rusted away and was also replaced, it is still displayed as the axe 'as used by George Washington'. The Mexuar, once a Muslim council chamber, was later a Catholic chapel, but now it is neither the one thing nor the other. Not only is the door not the original one (and we do not know where that door was), but the ceiling and the tiles on the walls are mostly post-Nasrid. The room has been extended towards the north, the west wall has been strengthened and windows have been added. Originally the room had a central lantern supported on four wooden columns to let in daylight. The floor was lowered sometime after 1492, possibly to reduce the danger of visitors falling out of the windows. A minstrel gallery was added when the place was used as a Catholic chapel, but then partially demolished. In the 1520s Charles V adorned one of the walls with a tiled representation of his emblem, the Pillars of Hercules, and his motto, 'PLUS ULTRA' (which can be translated as 'Beyond the Limit'), but that panel of tiles was subsequently moved from its original position to another wall. The capitals of the columns that support the low ceiling were repainted in the

1990s. The oratory, or prayer chamber, attached to the Mexuar was severely damaged in 1590 in a gunpowder-factory explosion and, though it has been restored, its restoration is anachronistic. Apart from all that, the Mexuar is just as the Nasrids left it and a place for tourists to marvel at.

The way in which the Mexuar has been restored has attracted criticism. This is also true of the site as a whole. Over the centuries bold architects and archaeologists have attempted to replace parts that were lost or fading. Often their restorations were based on nothing more than conjecture and prejudices reflecting the taste of the age. For instance, in 1858 Rafael Contreras, the architect who was first appointed to restore the palaces, decorated the eastern chamber of the Court of the Lions with tiles and added a dome in order to make it look more Persian, which was the way he thought it should look. In 1934 Torres Balbás attempted to put the matter right, but still got it wrong, as the roof he replaced it with is too steep and too high. Often lovingly executed restoration work has been just as carefully dismantled by a later generation of experts. The Alhambra is not a monument that is frozen in time; it is constantly being built and rebuilt. At the time of my last visit, in the spring of 2002, work in progress included restoration of a corner of the Court of the Myrtles, and the painted ceilings in the Hall of the Kings (Sala de los Reyes), and the whole of the Patio de la Acequia in the Generalife, as well as excavations in the Abencerrages ruins and the restoration of the Peinador Alto de la Reina (High Boudoir of the Queen, though prior to its use by Charles V's wife, Isabel, it was known as the Tower of Abu al-Juyush) . One of the rooms of the Palace of the Lions

6. An old photo shows the bogus Persian dome and crenellation that the imaginative architect Rafael Contreras added to the eastern pavilion in the Court of the Lions in 1858. Not only is Contreras's dome quite out of keeping with the Moorish architecture of the Alhambra, it does not even look authentically Persian. In 1934, the anachronistic dome was removed by another, slightly more punctilious restorer.

was also being restored. The church that stands on the site of the Nasrid mosque was closed for restoration. The way the Alhambra looks today owes more to modern craftsmanship than to medieval builders.

Nowadays the rooms and corridors of the palaces of the Alhambra are bare of furnishings and this must help speed the throughput of tourists, but of course, this was not always so. The medieval palaces were lavishly furnished with carpets, cushions and hangings. Descriptions of palaces in *The Arabian Nights* suggest that they were cluttered places. Curtains hung over doorways and peristyles. Carpets were hung out of windows (in much the same way that they were in Renaissance Venice, as can be seen, for example, in the paintings of Carpaccio). Carpets were also an essential part of picnic furniture and were regularly spread out in the gardens. (Since most of Nasrid court life was conducted seated on mats and cushions, the visitor should sit on the ground in order to see the buildings as the Moors saw them. The floor level existence of the Moors explains why the *miradors* and other windows tend to be set so low in the walls.) Movable furnishings and textiles played a large part in identifying the temporary functions of designated rooms. It was common for princes to employ a supervisor of textiles, the *Sahib al-Sitar*, to oversee their placement. The Alhambra affords a particularly striking example of what Lisa Golombek has called 'the draped universe of Islam'. When Ibn al-Khatib rhapsodised about the festivities that took place in 1362, he particularly stressed the splendid silk textiles that were laid out in the area of the Mexuar. His successor as vizier and court panegyrist, Ibn Zamrak, wrote in his *qasida* (ode) about the Court of the Lions, 'with how many fine draperies you have adorned it ... whose colourful embroidery makes us forget the Yemeni brocades'. The silk and wool textiles were probably produced by royal workshops within the palace city.

A significant number of the textiles that originally adorned the Alhambra have survived. Some of them bear the motto of the Nasrid sultans, '*La ghalib ila Allah*' ('No victor but God'). Spanish silks are among the most spectacular and pleasing examples of Islamic art. Although pre-Nasrid Spanish textiles often employed figurative imagery, Nasrid silks rely on austere, geometrical decoration and, in so doing, of course, they match the overall decorative schemes of the Alhambra. Wall hangings were designed to resemble stucco panels and vice versa. The stucco work often makes play with the polyphonic music of decorative interlace, as strap work is made to seem as if it is weaving over and under itself to cover the wall surface. Again, much of the ornament, particularly in the Cuarto Dorado and the Court of the Lions, seems to strive for the effect of weightlessness and is reminiscent of the decorative repertoire of lacework. On the other hand, the geometric patterns of some of the hangings mimic the structures of the palace's doors. One has to imagine brilliantly coloured carpets and silks blending in with the no less brilliantly coloured stucco and woodwork. Finally, it is worth remarking that, when Arab poets and writers wrote about the ornamentation of a building (in marble, tile, stone, stucco and so forth), they wrote of this ornamentation as metaphorically the 'apparel' of the building. The decorative inscriptions of the walls were referred to as *tiraz*, which is the term usually applied to decorative bands of embroidery attached to robes, especially court robes. It was common for poets to compare a lavishly decorated palace to a bride who has been made ready for her bridegroom. An inscription round a niche in the Sala de la Barca (Room of the Boat) begins 'Praise be to God. My finery and my diadem dazzle those already endowed with beauty ...'

Clearly the fourteenth-century Mexuar was even smaller and darker than it is today. More generally, nowhere in the palace complex is there much space for grand ceremonial and there are no sweeping vistas in the manner of Versailles. Muslim palaces were designed to give pleasure to their inhabitants, rather than to overawe the ruler's subjects. Such ostentation and pomp as there were in the Alhambra must have been on an intimate scale. This becomes yet more evident as one proceeds from the Mexuar into the Court of the Cuarto Dorado, or Golden Chamber. This court probably served as a kind of antechamber to the Comares Palace and it was here that the monarch, seated on a throne placed between the two doors on its southern wall, held public audience. That this was the place where the sovereign sat in state is indicated by the Throne verse of the Koran inscribed on the wall:

His Throne comprises the heavens and earth;
the preserving of them oppresses him not;
He is the All-high, the All-glorious.

Koran, 2:256

It is also likely that its southern wall was the façade of the Comares Palace. The façade is magnificently decorated in carved stucco, and yet that magnificence and that of the Court of the Cuarto Dorado as a whole is on an intimate scale. It is the detail of the decoration rather than the expanse

[34]

it covers that suggests infinity. The decoration of the lower part of this façade is the work of modern restorers. By the early nineteenth century the original stucco had fallen off, revealing the underlying rough stonework. While one of the two doors leads on into the Comares Palace, the other merely takes one back to the forecourts of the palace. According to Dickie, this second door originally led nowhere and was there to confuse a potential assassin. This does not seem very likely, for the would-be assassin would have to be pretty dim to be so easily flummoxed (and an attentive reading of the history of the Nasrids suggests that the would-be assassin usually got his man). It is more probable that considerations of symmetry led to the provision of two doors on this wall. Like the Mexuar, the Cuarto Dorado has been heavily restored (and the upper storey of the Golden Chamber was destroyed by Ferdinand and Isabella). However, the restoration here has been less controversial.

In his *Tales of the Alhambra*, the nineteenth-century American writer Washington Irving (on whom see Chapter 4) described the passage from the Cuarto Dorado into the Court of the Myrtles in the following terms:

> *The transition was almost magical; it seemed as if we were at once transported into othertimes and another realm, were treading the scenes of Arabian story. We found ourselves in a great court, paved with white marble and decorated at each end with light Moorish peristyles ... In the centre was an immense basin or fish-pond, a hundred and thirty feet in length by thirty in breadth, stocked with gold-fish and bordered by hedges of roses. At the upper end of this court rose the great Tower of Comares.*

7. The Court of the Myrtles looking north towards the Comares Tower and the Hall of the Ambassadors. The myrtle beds that line the pool would originally have been sunken, so as to allow a clear view of the water from the sides.

Although the Court of the Myrtles was originally built by Yusuf I, most of what now stands is actually the work of Muhammad V (and of course subsequent assorted builders, vandals and restoration experts). At the north end, the Comares Tower looms over the courtyard and the pool. The gallery at the south end nestles in the shadow of Charles V's monumental Renaissance palace to which it has been joined. The east and west sides have five doorways each, leading into small, fairly austere rooms. In the centre of the court is a long pool flanked by myrtles. Until Rafael Contreras did restoration work there in the early nineteenth century, the garden was paved with tombstones plundered from Muslim cemeteries.

The anachronistic rose bushes recorded by Washington Irving in the early nineteenth century have also since been removed. The original garden did contain myrtle bushes, as well as orange trees, as the Venetian ambassador Andrea Navagiero, who toured the Alhambra in the early sixteenth century, testifies. The great North African philosopher-historian Ibn Khaldun spent the years 1363 to 1365 in Granada, from where he went on missions for Muhammad V and maintained friendly if rather strained relations with the vizier, Ibn al-Khatib. Later in his masterpiece on the philosophy of history, the *Muqaddima*, Ibn Khaldun wrote of orange trees as a sign of social decadence: 'This is the meaning of the statement by certain knowing people, that if orange trees are much grown in a town, the town invites its own ruin.' Not, Ibn Khaldun hastened to add, that orange trees are a bad omen or anything like that, but they are, like cypress trees, a sign of a sedentary culture. Such trees produce no edible fruit, but are planted only for the sake of their

8. The Court of the Myrtles, looking south, as rendered by the nineteenth-century artist John Frederick Lewis. Though it is not clear in this picture, the Palace of Charles V looms over the southern end of the Court of the Myrtles.

appearance. They are a sign of the diversification of luxuries that is characteristic of a dynasty or race that has become sedentarised. Once rulers have achieved power, they seek to relax: 'They plant gardens and enjoy life.' However, one may be sure that within three generations at most, they will have lost all that their ancestors conquered. Ibn Khaldun's bizarrely sombre meditations on orange trees were a tiny part of his much grander philosophy of history, which dealt with the cyclical rise and fall of dynasties and the role of nomads as violent agents of change. When Ibn Khaldun described the orange as inedible, he was not being faddy about his food; he was writing about the Seville orange, which is indeed bitter and is used as an acid element in cooking. The sweet orange originated in the Far East and was introduced to Europe and the Middle East by the Portuguese in the sixteenth century. In a further postscript, it is perhaps worth mentioning that Dick Davis, the Arabist and poet, clearly read Ibn Khaldun on this topic and was inspired to write a poem, entitled 'The City of Orange Trees', which begins,

> The city filled with orange trees
> Is lost, which, interpreted, meant
> All conspicuous luxuries
> Augur ruinous punishment.

Although Irving tells us he went swimming in the pool of the Court of the Myrtles, there is very little evidence that any medieval Muslims took such exercise. In the eighth century the ill-fated Umayyad prince Walid built the desert palace of Khirbat al-Mafjar in the Jordan valley, which included a large music room with a swimming pool in it. In an adjoining room Walid also had a smaller pool that was filled with wine and he used to immerse himself in it while listening to the singers he had summoned to entertain him. In sixteenth-century India, Babur, the founder of the Mughal dynasty, delighted in swimming across the Ganges and other Indian rivers, and sometimes he was drunk or on dope when he did so. Otherwise references to Muslims swimming for pleasure are almost unknown in medieval times. Though *hammam*s (baths) were an important feature of Islamic palaces and were used for ritual ablutions as well as in the interests of ordinary cleanliness, Muslims did not favour immersion baths. Why swim in one's own dirt? As we shall see, when Charles V decided to live in the Alhambra, he had one of the *hammam*s modified so that he could bathe in the Western style.

Having described the Court of the Myrtles, Irving went on to elaborate fantasies of those 'other times', with tales of sultans, viziers, princesses, astrologers and sighing lovers. The use of architecture and especially ruined architecture as a peg for meditations on mortality, transience and the mysteries of the past is a commonplace of literature and popular history writing. In his *Autobiography*, the historian G. M. Trevelyan wrote of the latent romance of past times:

> *The poetry of history lies in the quasi miraculous fact that once, on this earth, once on this familiar spot of ground, walked other men and women, as actual as we are today, thinking their own thoughts, swayed by their own passions, but now all gone, one generation vanishing into another, gone as utterly as we ourselves shall shortly be gone, like ghosts at cockcrow.*

This is eloquently put, but in the case of the Alhambra there are quite a few obstacles that get in the way of conjuring up the ghosts of those who originally dwelt there. As one stands in the Court of the Myrtles and contemplates the reflected buildings wavering in the waters of the long pool, one may have the illusion that one is standing in a medieval palace that has miraculously withstood the ravages of time and that at any moment the place will come alive with court functionaries, servants, guards and veiled women going about their business. But it is an illusion. As is the case with the Mexuar, what one now sees is not exactly what was once there. First, though the flanking of the watercourse with myrtle bushes is authentic, the beds of myrtles would have been sunk a metre deep, so as not to impede the view of the water. Secondly, according to the Venetian Andrea Navagiero, in the early sixteenth century the surrounding surface was paved in white marble. There were also orange trees in the courtyard. The Comares Tower on the north side of the courtyard did not originally have crenellations or a turret and, of course, neither was the south gallery overshadowed by Charles V's palace (the construction of which began in the 1520s). Then one must also bear in mind that the present slightly austere look of the Comares Palace complex is somewhat misleading, for this and the other palaces would have been richly furnished with textiles.

The Sala de la Barca is on the north side of the Court of Myrtles. It is situated behind the gallery and leads into the Hall of the Ambassadors. According to most guidebooks, it takes its name from the Spanish for 'boat' as the ceiling could be thought to be shaped like the hull of a boat. However, Dickie has suggested that really the name is a corruption of *baraka*, the Arabic word for 'blessing'. This is probably correct as the lengthy inscription over the portico preceding the Sala de la Barca begins as follows: 'Blessed be He who has entrusted you with the command of his servants and who through you has exalted [the world of Islam] and its benefits …' Dickie has also argued that the Sala de la Barca was a bedroom, but the room is awkwardly shaped for this purpose and, besides, it is extremely badly placed to be a bedroom, as it leads directly into a public audience chamber. It is more plausible that it was a dining room, though there is no evidence for this either. The room, and especially the ceiling, has been extensively restored after a fire in 1890. The barred doorway one sees on the east side that leads into the Hall of the Ambassadors was originally not a doorway but a *mihrab* (prayer niche indicating the direction in which a Muslim should pray). However, Torres Balbás, who undertook restoration work in the 1930s and 1940s, mistook it for a doorway and made an entrance where there was none before – one instance among many where the archaeologists and art historians have done more harm than good.

Set in the walls of the entrance arch of the Sala de la Barca there are niches, and there are other similar niches elsewhere throughout the palaces. These would have framed vases or jars, that might have contained water, though probably the vases had a mainly decorative function. Other vases were placed in the corners of rooms as display ware. The so-called 'Alhambra vases' are the most spectacular examples of decorative ceramics produced as architectural accessories in the fourteenth and fifteenth centuries. They are thick-walled amphorae with handles like wings and are about 120–130 centimetres high and thus too large for most niches. At least ten such vases have survived. Their lustre decoration is exquisite. The 'Jar of the Gazelles' in the Alhambra Museum, a particularly fine piece of work, is decorated in gold, white and blue, which seem to have been the dynastic colours of the Nasrids. The sixteenth-century Emperor Rudolf II prided himself on possessing one of the wine jars used at the wedding at Cana on the occasion when Jesus turned water into wine. Rudolf kept it in his cabinet of curiosities, but actually his jar was one of the Alhambra vases.

The Sala de la Barca leads into the Hall of the Ambassadors. This imposing space is unmistakably a throne room and audience chamber. The windowed alcove opposite the entrance is the recess where the throne would have been placed. This alcove is flanked by two more whose windows also offer spectacular views over the Rio Darro and across to Albaicín. Indeed, the Hall of the Ambassadors has been described as 'a dilated mirador' (by James Dickie). From this hall the sultan's gaze comprehended his lands and subjects.

Under the dome of the hall one finds Sura 67 of the Koran, entitled *Al-Mulk*, or 'Kingdom', which begins as follows:

> Blessed be He in whose hand is the Kingdom –
> He is powerful over everything –
> who created death and life, that He might try you
> which of you is fairest in works; and He is
> the All-mighty, the All-forgiving –
> who created seven heavens one upon another ...
> Thou seest not in the creation
> Of the All-mighty any imperfection.
> Return thy gaze; seest thou any fissure?
> Then return thy gaze again, and thy gaze comes

Back to thee dazzled aweary.
And we adorned the lower heavens with lamps and
made them
Things to stone Satans; and We have prepared for them
The chastisement of the Blaze.

In the context of the Hall of the Ambassadors, the Koranic verses can be read as alluding to the majesty of kingship and hinting at a symbolic reading of the ceiling. This is an intricately patterned example of marquetry and is composed of over 8,000 pieces of cedarwood. Twelve-sided stars are the main feature of the pattern and the ceiling with its seven levels of differing stylised star patterns can be 'read' as a geometric representation of the seven heavens in microcosm. The Hall of the Ambassadors is not now as it once was. For one thing, the wooden ceiling was originally painted in a range of bright colours (and the survival of a carpenter's note on the back of one of the pieces of wood allows one to reconstruct some of the vanished polychromy of the ceiling). The stained glass in the windows was destroyed in the 1590 gunpowder explosion, while the windows on one of the walls were bricked up to prevent its collapse. Also it seems probable that the whole floor was originally paved in small lustreware tiles. Muslims would have entered the hall barefoot, but such an extravagant flooring would soon have been worn out by the boots of the Christians. Today only a small central area of the hall is still covered in tiles, not all of which are original. As for those that do appear to be original, they pose a problem, as several bear the inscription '*La ghalib ila Allah*' ('No victor but God'). This piece of calligraphy served as both the motto and the heraldic device of the Nasrid dynasty, but surely no good Muslim would have dreamt of treading on a tile on which 'Allah' featured?

It is probable that there was a chamber on the south side of the Court of the Myrtles that corresponded to and was similar to the Sala de la Barca, but whatever was once there was demolished so that Charles V could connect his palace to the Nasrid palace. It has been suggested that the small windowless rooms on the east and west sides of the Court of the Myrtles were the apartments of the royal harem. Although this is quite plausible, there is absolutely no evidence for it and these rooms could equally well have been offices used by bureaucrats. We simply do not know how this place was inhabited. In fact, it was not all that common for rooms in Islamic palaces to have specialised functions. Reflecting on an Arab account of the tour of a Byzantine embassy round an Abbasid palace in Baghdad in the early tenth century, the distinguished historian of Islamic art Oleg Grabar noted (in *The Formation of Islamic Art*) that only one hall, the Official Gate, had a fixed single function: 'All other units were prepared for the occasion. It may be concluded that these palaces did not have functionally defined forms and that human activity determined the function of a given space ...' He also observed that the Arab account focused on the furnishings and treasures displayed in the rooms of the palace rather than the rooms themselves, so that 'the building was not an end in itself but a flexible support like a frame, like the stage of a theatre, whose visible aspect could be modified to suit the need of the moment'.

The Alhambra's baths are situated on the eastern edge of the Court of the Myrtles and are connected to it and to the Court of the Lions, but on a lower level. They were probably built by Ismail I (1314–25), with later additions by his son Yusuf I. The complex, lit by overhead windows, included hot, warm and cold rooms, changing room cum rest room (with a lavatory annexe) and furnaces and a wood store. It is possible that these baths, like Roman baths, may have served as a place for the conduct of business and for socialising. However, the religious function of the *hammam* was almost certainly more important. In order to perform the prayer, a Muslim has to be in a state of ritual purity. The *wudu*, or lesser ablution, has to be performed after defecating, urinating or sleeping. In the lesser ablution, the face, head, arms up to the elbows and feet have to be washed in a ritualised order and this could be conveniently performed at a basin or courtyard fountain, such as that in the Court of the Lions. However, the *ghusl*, or complete washing of the body, is obligatory after warfare, sex or the emission of semen, and one would usually have recourse to a *hammam* for this. Fantasies of odalisques and lolling sensualists eating grapes and eyeing each others' bodies are almost certainly inappropriate. Visits to the *hammam* were single-sex affairs, and those who used the baths draped their private parts with towels. Since all the Muslims in the Alhambra would have been obliged to have recourse to a *hammam*, there were also several public baths within the palace city.

Muslims perform the ablutions by pouring water over themselves. Once again what you see in the *hammam* today is not exactly what was once there. Since there was no bath in the palace that Pedro Machuca was building from the late 1520s onwards, Charles V continued to use the old Moorish *hammam*, but as he was accustomed to the Western style of bathing, he installed an immersion bath in the hot room and added his 'PLUS ULTRA' emblem to the wall. In the nineteenth century Contreras undertook a vigorous and confident programme of restoration, in the course of which he removed Charles's emblem, repainted the place and rearranged the inscriptions. Since he relied on Owen Jones and Jules Goury's book about the Alhambra and its (inaccurate) registration of the colours of the paintwork in the *hammam*, he had the place painted in anachronistically lurid hues. (On Jones and Goury, see Chapter 4.) As for the inscriptions, Contreras, who knew no Arabic, rearranged them in such a way that it is no longer possible to make sense of them. In recent decades the baths have also suffered from damp.

THE COURT OF THE LIONS

No building work of any significance was undertaken by the Nasrids during the politically turbulent period from 1354 to 1362, and when it recommenced it was in quite a different style. Nowadays the tourist route takes one directly from the Court of the Myrtles to the Palace and Court of the Lions, but this was not originally the case. In Nasrid times the Palace of the Lions was an entirely separate building that was reached only from the street. The two buildings were joined together only in the reign of Ferdinand and Isabella. 'Palace of the Lions' is a modern label and derives from the stone lions that support the basin of the fountain in the centre of the courtyard. We have so very few sources about life in late fourteenth-century Granada that we cannot be certain what this place was originally called. James Dickie has argued from an inscription over the Mirador of Lindaraxa, that since the inscription refers to the window as *'Ayn dar 'Aisha* or 'Eye of the Palace of 'Aisha', the palace must have originally been named after an 'Aisha who would have been one of Sultan Muhammad V's wives. However, we do not know what any of the sultan's wives were called and, moreover, Fernández-Puertas is no less confident that this complex of buildings was known as the Palace of the Riyad. *Riyad* means 'gardens' or 'cemeteries'. He deduces this from one of the poems in Ibn Zamrak's collections of poems, in which the poet seems to refer to the place as the Riyad, and from the inscription composed by him that runs round the walls of the Hall of the Two Sisters and begins: '*Ana al-rawd*' (I am the gardens). Moreover, the building did indeed overlook the Nasrid royal cemetery. However, both Dickie and Fernández-Puertas may be wrong, and as we shall see (in Chapter 3), it is possible that the Palace of the Lions was not a palace at all. In the meantime we may ask: why build yet another palace? Did not Muhammad V already have enough palaces? Some scholars have suggested the Comares Palace was the public palace where the sultan exercised his functions as ruler, whereas the Court of the Lions was the private palace reserved for the sultan and his harem. It is possible, though there is no particular evidence for this.

After the return of Muhammad V and his court from exile in Fez, a big party to mark the birth of the Prophet was held in December 1362 on the future site of the Court of the Lions. Among other things this was an opportunity to show off recent building work, though, of the Court of the Lions complex, only the Hall of the Two Sisters had been built by the end of 1362. The sultan had most of his father's Mexuar demolished and rebuilt in time for this festivity. There was feasting and sermons, poetry recitation, dancing and displays of horsemanship. Building work began soon afterwards. It is worth stressing that the vizier and poet Ibn al-Khatib's contemporary account of those festivities, though somewhat vague and open to various readings, is just about the only written source on how any part of the Alhambra was used prior to 1492. Though there is much of technical and historical interest to be said about the Court of the Lions, the first thing to be remarked is that it is, by common consent, one of the most beautiful buildings in the world and there are many who would even go beyond that qualified judgement. The proportions and the delicacy and elaboration of the ornamentation of the architecture are breathtaking (and the effect is redoubled if one enters the courtyard by moonlight). One has a sense of the architecture descending from heaven rather than resting upon the earth on which it was built. The screens of insubstantial-looking stonework receding into the shadows produce a strikingly stereoscopic effect. At the centre of the courtyard there is a basin that appears to be supported by twelve stone lions that double as water spouts. The stone lions, gazing blindly into the sun, do not actually support the fountain, though. The four water channels run from the fountain to divide the courtyard into four quadrants, each of which is twice as long as it is wide. There is an intimate feel to the place. Dickie has suggested that this was a Moorish version of a rural villa in the middle of a town (*'rus in urbe'*).

Despite the extraordinary abundance of intricate decoration, there is a faintly austere feel to the Court of the Lions and Michael Jacobs (the author of several excellent books on Andalusia) has compared it to a Zen rock garden. It was not always so. The current, pleasing sandstone look of the place, with touches of faded paint only here and there, is quite false to the medieval original. In the fourteenth century the stone, wood and stucco were gaudily painted in blue and gold and other colours, brilliant carpets and hangings were disposed around the courtyard and, in place of the present pebbled surface, many would argue, the centre of the Court of the Lions was a garden filled with flowers and orange trees. The garden would have been a sunken one, so that the carpet of flowers did not impede the view of the fountain. Four raised walkways of stone would have then converged on the fountain. An account of the Court of the Lions in 1602 indicates that each quadrant of the courtyard contained six orange trees, growing amid flowers. It has further been argued that the shape of the garden, a rectangle divided by four water channels, was based upon the *chahar-bagh*, the traditional 'fourfold plot' Persian garden design. From this point of view, it is possible to imagine that the buildings were hardly more than a frame for the luxuriant garden.

The present administration of the Alhambra, the Patronato de la Alhambra, resists demands for the restoration of the hypothetical garden, on the quite reasonable grounds that such a garden and the rising damp brought on by its irrigation would do long-term damage to the foundations of the buildings around it. What's more, there may not have been a garden there in Moorish times after all. In an article published in Spanish a few decades ago Enrique Nuere Matauco argued that in the fourteenth and fifteenth centuries the courtyard was devoid of vegetation, but was paved in marble. He based his argument on the testimony of the German traveller Hieronymus Münzer about his tour of the Alhambra in 1494. Münzer was enthusiastic about the

Alhambra and especially the marble covering of the court-yard with the fountain. He did not believe that its equal was to be found anywhere in Europe. It seems that only in the nineteenth century did it become a garden. Richard Ford, who visited the Alhambra in the 1840s, criticised the authorities for having made the courtyard into a garden *a la francesa* and having sold off the original paving. In the Court of the Lions 'ill-usage has done its worst; the roof is modern and was put on … in 1770. The cockney garden is French, the whitewashings and repairs Spanish.' What is most telling is the way in which we are so heavily dependent on the descriptions of Western visitors in order to reconstruct the way the place once looked. Ibn al-Khatib, Ibn Zamrak and quite a few other Arab writers celebrated the palace in copious verse and prose, but always in effusively slippery generalities. The literary courtiers of the Nasrids were masters of the pleasing cliché.

The original entrance on the façade of the south side of the Court of the Lions, where the foundation inscription of the building would have been, was destroyed in order to link the building with Charles V's palace. The chamber that survives on the south side of the Court of the Lions is known, for no good reason, as the Hall of the Abencerrages. The tile work of the chamber is not original but dates from the sixteenth or seventeenth century. The Hall of the Abencerrages was more enclosed then (and it still possesses its large wooden door) and it was therefore habitable in the winter. The marble fountain in the centre is stained red, and in the early nineteenth century Irving was told that the stain was that of the Banu Sarraj, a powerful clan of courtiers, many of whom were victims of a massacre in the fifteenth century.

Guides have continued to relate 'the ancient tale of blood and violence' ever since.

The lions at the centre of the courtyard are not realistically sculpted. According to the nineteenth-century travel writer Richard Ford, their 'faces are barbecued, and their manes cut like scales of a griffin, and their legs like bedposts, while a water-pipe stuck in their mouths does not add to their dignity'. They were once brightly painted. Contrary to what many of the guidebooks claim, they almost certainly date from the fourteenth century, not the eleventh. In the Museum of the Alhambra there are two similarly unrealistic stone lions that might have been carved by the same hand and which once stood in the grounds of a *maristan*, or hospital, that was founded by Muhammad V in Albaicín, across the valley from the Alhambra. However, those lions that used to guard the hospital and spout water are almost 1.5 metres high and they are in a squatting rather than a standing position. An inscription composed by the poet Ibn Zamrak runs round the edge of the fountain in the Court of the Lions: 'In appearance liquid and solid appear to be fused, so that we do not know which of the two is moving.' He also composed a poem that accurately describes how the fountain functioned at the heart of what he called the 'Dar al-Riyad'.

These days the tourist, proceeding from the Comares Palace, enters the Court of the Lions complex on the west side, through the Hall of the Mocárabes. However, there was originally no connecting door between the two palaces and the main façade of the Court of the Lions was on the south side. The long Hall of the Mocárabes takes its name from the *muqarnas* ceiling, which it no longer possesses. The ceiling that we see today is not the original one, as this was badly damaged in the gunpowder explosion in 1590 and replaced in the seventeenth century. *Muqarnas* refers to the system of projecting niches used for zones of transition and for architectural decoration and its use produces those stalactitic and honeycomb effects that are so characteristic of the Alhambra. *Muqarnas* originated, apparently independently, in northeastern Iran in the tenth century and in eleventh-century North Africa. Mocárabes is the style of *muqarnas* favoured in the western Islamic world and it will be discussed more fully below, when we come to the Hall of the Two Sisters. Although *muqarnas* has been used by architects throughout most of the Muslim world (and there are, for instance, some particularly magnificent examples to be found in Iranian monuments), the Spanish and North African way of working with honeycomb effects has exercised a particularly strong influence on Western architects and designers who have sought to incorporate orientalising designs and motifs. Fantasy mock oriental architecture, as found in Britain, the United States and elsewhere, has tended to draw upon the Alhambra for its arches and ceilings and on India for its domes and minarets.

Facing the Hall of the Mocárabes, on the east side of the Court of Lions, is the Hall of Kings, within which square and rectangular spaces alternate. The most striking feature of this area is the ceiling vaults covered with paintings done in gesso on leather, and featuring men, women and other figurative imagery. There is no certainty about what is represented in these paintings or who did them. The great (if somewhat crazy) Orientalist Louis Massignon argued that they were the work of Muslim artists, but other scholars see these paintings as being firmly in the Western tradition. Indeed there was hardly a tradition of figurative painting in Muslim Andalusia. Only one illustrated manuscript survives from the whole period of Moorish rule in Spain. It has therefore been suggested that Muhammad V may have borrowed painters from his political ally, Pedro the Cruel of Castile. The ten seated men portrayed on the roof of the central alcove may be the first ten rulers of the Nasrid dynasty. (But this would be impossible if the painting was done in the reign of Muhammad V, as he was only the eighth of his line.) On the other hand, they may represent great sages or famous writers. The most cogent reading of the imagery of the paintings on the side vaults has been provided by the American art historian Jerrilynn Dodds, who argues that all the paintings were done by Muslim slaves sent by Pedro. She suggests that the artists may have been acquainted with Christian and vaguely Arthurian motifs from European romances as depicted, for example, on French ivory caskets, but that they were not very familiar with them. Therefore they jumbled motifs from various romances together in such a manner that there is no overall story to be 'read' in the paintings.

On the north side of the courtyard is the Hall of the Two Sisters, which, as we have already noted, was the only part of the Court of the Lions complex to have been built by 1362. There is no more logic to its name than there is to the names of the other components of the Court of the Lions. 'Two Sisters' refers to the two great slabs of marble set in the floor. Like the Hall of the Abencerrages, the Hall of the Two Sisters originally possessed a vast door, but that door has been moved to the Museum of the Alhambra. The hall also had stained-glass windows, but these were destroyed in the gunpowder explosion of 1590. In other respects the hall has survived fairly well. Its *muqarnas* ceiling, a *tour de force* geometer's art, is composed of over 5,000 prismatic pie... Seven basic prism shapes, all in stucco, have been used. The function of the *muqarnas* here is to mediate between the octagonal drum of the ceiling and the rectangular shape of the chamber below. The ceiling seems to float over the hall without receiving support from the walls; the overall effect is of a celestial explosion.

Its spectacular decorative effect apart, the *muqarnas* ceiling may have had an acoustic function. It is quite possible that Koran recitals, concerts and soirées were held in this hall. The ribbed ceiling would have been effective in reducing echo. There seems to have been a long tradition of designing chambers that would be suitable for royal concerts. According to Robert Hamilton's magisterial survey of the eighth-century Syrian Umayyad palace of Khirbat al-Mafjar, its music room had a series of semicircular apses capped by semi-domes and the 'reflecting concavities of these structures, with the dome above the central square, were designed to flatter the voice of a singer shrewd enough to place himself on the central carpet, the position designed for him'.

An intervening chamber links the Hall of the Sisters with the Lindaraxa. The latter is a richly decorated belvedere. Its name is a Spanish distortion of the Arabic *'Ayn dar 'Aisha*. The conceit is the geminate window representing the eye of the ruler, who here may gaze on the lands he rules. 'In this garden I am an eye filled with delight and the pupil of this eye is none other than our lord ... In me he looks from his caliphal throne towards the capital of his entire kingdom', according to an inscription composed for the site by Ibn Zamrak. This is a typical example of Ibn Zamrak's use of

e for boasting (in Arabic, *fakhr*). It is also an
n flattery, as Muhammad V had no claims to
aliph, or spiritual head of the Sunni Muslim
lly one looked out from the belvedere on to an
garden and from there across to the Albaicín.
as curtailed when Charles V decided to have his
residen apartments built around the north and east sides
of the much diminished Lindaraxa garden.

GARDENS AND LOST PALACES

The architecture of the Lindaraxa was subordinate to the
view it commanded. Within the Court of the Lions itself the
distinction between exterior and interior is elided as water
channels run from the central fountain into the rooms on the
east and west sides. More generally, the architects of the
Alhambra worked with the gardens, water and light. Robert
Hillenbrand has eloquently described this interplay of the
elements:

*The Alhambra brings the forces of nature into play at every turn:
water in movement – trickling, running, cascading, spurting –
or still, in tranquil expanses: carefully barbered trees and bushes;
sunken flower beds; sudden glimpses of mountains or gardens
framed in a casement, or, more ambitiously, miradors and
belvederes cunningly placed to exploit sight lines over an entire
landscape; and above all light. The Alhambra studiously manip-
ulates contrasts of light and dark, with bent entrances, shafts of
sunlight angled into shadowy interiors, dim passageways suddenly opening into a courtyard open to the blazing sun, and light
reflected from placid ponds or walls clad in glistening tiles.*

The openness of the buildings of the Alhambra, the inter-penetration of interior and exterior spaces and the flexible use of space all prefigure the work of Le Corbusier. (Early on in his career, the Swiss architect had discovered in the Alhambra 'the intelligent, just and magnificent interplay of volumes made harmonious by daylight'.)

Rawda means 'garden', but, as already noted, it also means cemetery. The Nasrid cemetery with its canopy tombs was located to the south of the Court of the Lions. It was probably founded by Ismail I but was mostly destroyed to make room for Charles V's palace, and the funerary stones were used for other things. Several of the original royal tomb-stones, slabs of white marble, are now in the Museum of the Alhambra. In the Muslim world cemeteries, with cypresses, myrtles and other plants, were popular places for picnics and musical entertainments. Presumably the sense of transience afforded by such a site gave a pleasingly melancholy edge to the picnickers' enjoyment. The earthly funerary garden pre-sented an image of the paradise to come. According to a saying of the Prophet, 'Between my tomb and my pulpit there is a garden [*rawda*] which is one of the gardens of Paradise.'

It is likely that the Royal Great Mosque, built in the years 1303–5 by Muhammad III on a site to the south of the cem-etery, was the most spectacular building within the Alhambra complex. Ibn al-Khatib composed a poem that celebrated its extravagant marble, mosaics and silver lamps. Sadly, it no longer exists as it was destroyed in the 1560s in order to make space for the rather ugly Church of Santa Maria de la Alhambra which covers most of its foundations. Only the bath of the mosque, which was restored by Torres Balbás in 1934, survives.

One last palace needs to be mentioned, the Palace of the Conde de Tendilla, but it is hard to do more than mention it, as it no longer exists. This was located some way to the south-east of the Partal Palace. A palace was first built here by Muhammad II, but it was extensively rebuilt by Yusuf III (r. 1408–17). It seems to have consisted of a series of pavilions round a central pool. Münzer seems to have thought it the most splendid of all the palaces. It was chosen by the counts of Tendilla, the hereditary governors of the Alhambra under the Catholic monarchs, to be their residence. However, when in 1717 the Marquis of Mondéjar, the heir of the counts of Tendilla, was deposed from his office by Philip V, he demolished his palace. (A fit of pique?)

In addition to the palaces, the Alhambra once had at least thirty towers spread along the walls at irregular intervals, but only twenty-two survive. Ferdinand and Isabella reduced the height of some of these towers so that they would be less vulnerable to artillery. Most of them had purely military functions, but two are, in fact, small palaces. The Torre de la Cautiva, also known as the Qalahurra Nueva of Yusuf I, is sited on the outer defence wall of the Alhambra east of the Partal. The Tower of the Captive Princess is an entirely fanciful name. Ibn al-Jayyab, Yusuf I's vizier and Ibn al-Khatib's predecessor as court poet, referred to the building in a contemporary inscription on its walls as a Qalahurra. (A *qalahurra* was a military-tower dwelling.) Its stucco and tile work is similar to that of the Court of the Myrtles, which Yusuf I also inaugurated. At some point in its history the tower was damaged by fire and acquired a nineteenth-century floor and ceiling. Similarly the next tower along from Yusuf's tower, the Qalahurra Nueva of Muhammad VII, has been romantically named the Tower of the Princesses. It was probably (though not certainly) built at the end of the fourteenth century and, if that dating is right, it is the last significant example of building work in the Moorish Alhambra complex. The tower-residence seems to have been loosely modelled on the Hall of the Two Sisters, but it lost its original *muqarnas* vault in an earthquake. Some have detected decadence in the poverty of its ornamentation. According to Fernández-Puertas, 'With its ponderous architectural forms, uninspired ornament and dominance of plain surfaces, it shows an astonishing decline in little over twenty years.' However, this is very much in the eye of the beholder and in the past the place has been much admired. Neither of the two towers is usually open to tourists. Nor are the upstairs rooms of the Court of the Myrtles and the Court of the Lions, nor the baths. As we have seen, other monuments cannot be visited because they no longer exist. Those who visit the Alhambra today need to be aware that what they see is only a small part of what was standing in 1492. Three of the palaces have vanished altogether, as has the Great Mosque, together with the busy commercial and industrial zone to the east of the main cluster of palaces. It is one thing to summon up in one's imagination the princes, courtiers and sentries of past centuries; it is another to conjure up the ghosts of buildings.

Gardens were outdoor extensions of the buildings, many of which were only built to frame the views of those gardens. Though they are indeed delightful, the gardens of the Alhambra and Generalife reflect the horticultural tastes of Spain in the 1920s, rather than medieval realities. It seems most probable that, for the medieval visitors and inhabitants of the Alhambra, the gardens took precedence over the buildings that were set among them, but it is no longer possible to reconstruct the original appearance of the gardens, except in the broadest outline. Much of the vegetation that one sees here today was unknown to the Moors and, among other things, they tended not to plant flowers in beds. They preferred to scatter them throughout the grass. Moreover, it seems likely that large areas would have been set aside for kitchen-gardening and the pasturage of horses.

The gardens of the Generalife were not connected to the palaces in Moorish times, so that when the sultan chose to visit his estate there, he would have actually ridden across from the Alhambra. The garden, which very likely served as a place to escape from state business, was probably established in the opening decades of the fourteenth century. Although the derivation of Generalife from *Janna al-'Arif*, meaning 'Garden of the Architect', or, perhaps, 'Garden of the Gnostic', has become a hallowed piece of lore, this is etymologically unlikely. We do not know why the garden acquired this name. In fact it seems to have been originally called 'Principal Orchard'. The only substantial part of the garden that has survived in a fashion is the Patio de la Acequia, or Water Garden Courtyard, with its North Pavilion and Dismounting Yard. Like the Court of the Myrtles, the patio has a long central water channel. The fountains that play over it are probably anachronistic, as Muslims do not seem to have favoured jet fountains. (However, by the early sixteenth century when Navagiero visited the garden, jet fountains were in place.) The buildings round the pool were extensively reconstructed after 1492 and the *mirador* converted into a chapel, as Ferdinand and

9. The Patio de la Acequia (Water Garden Courtyard) in the gardens of the Generalife. For pious Muslims, such gardens and pavilions evoked thoughts of Paradise as described in the Koran. Though the medieval Muslim designers frequently placed fountains in buildings and gardens, they tended to favour overflow fountains rather than projectile ones. Therefore, the jets of water seen here may have been first installed by the Catholic monarchs after 1492.

Isabella were very fond of the Generalife. Several sixteenth-century visitors to Granada were more impressed by the gardens than by the palaces. During restoration work on the Patio de la Acequia the year after a fire in 1958, the layout of the original garden, together with its still intact irrigation system, was uncovered. These the 'restorers' promptly destroyed. The garden originally had a cruciform design with flowerbeds sunken below the walkways. Of the upper level, only the delightful water stairway survives close by. This stairway, whose stone banisters carry streams of water, seems to have led to an oratory that has since vanished.

THE ALHAMBRA OF THE CHRISTIAN KINGS

After 1492 the Alhambra was designated a royal palace, a status that it retained until 1868. When Ferdinand and Isabella moved in, they found the palaces sadly run down and they recruited Muslim craftsmen to do restoration work (and such craftsmen were required again, when in 1522 an earthquake damaged the Court of the Lions). In 1495 the Catholic monarchs gave the site of a Nasrid palace to the Franciscans for their convent and later in the sixteenth century a church replaced the mosque. Juana, the daughter of Ferdinand and Isabella, inherited Castile as well as an enthusiasm for the Moorish palaces, which she passed on to her son Charles, who became King of Spain in 1516 and Holy Roman Emperor in 1519.

As King of Spain, Charles V possessed a great empire in the New World and he also ruled over the Netherlands, Naples, Sicily and Sardinia. His 'PLUS ULTRA' motto boasted of his ambition to travel and conquer beyond the Pillars of

Hercules, even to the ends of the earth. He was a Catholic zealot and his first act upon entering Granada in 1526 was to order in the Inquisition to hunt out crypto-Muslims who had only pretended to convert to Christianity. Even so he was also an enthusiast for Moorish architecture. When he first entered the magnificent eleventh-century Great Mosque of Cordoba and saw the grotesque Catholic chapel that the priests had plonked in the middle of the forest of Moorish arches, he expostulated, 'You have built what you or others might have built anywhere, but you have destroyed something that was unique in the world.' His visit to Granada in 1526 was also his honeymoon and he and his bride, Isabel of Portugal, lodged in the Alhambra (in the part of the palace later inhabited by Washington Irving).

Having looked round the Alhambra, Charles delivered his verdict on Boabdil's abdication: 'Had I been he or he been I, I would rather have made this place my sepulchre.' However, though he certainly admired the place, it was not very convenient for holding large state functions or receiving and lodging foreign missions and, besides, it was very cold in winter. He promptly commissioned the architect Pedro Machuca to build him a modern palace in the Renaissance style within the grounds of the Alhambra. Machuca had previously trained as a painter and worked in Italy with Raphael and Michelangelo. After Machuca's death in 1550, a succession of other architects laboured to complete the work, and it dragged on for a century before being abandoned. Since the roof was never completed, the building deteriorated quite rapidly. The place was used as a storage yard for gunpowder and other materials. During the Peninsular War, the French, mostly bivouacked in the convent of San Francisco, stripped what woodwork they could find in the palace for their fires. Work on the palace commissioned by Charles in 1526 was completed only in the twentieth century.

Although the clashes in style and scale between Charles's palace and the Nasrid palaces on which it abuts are glaring, nevertheless the Renaissance building is a magnificent work of architecture in its own right. Richard Ford, who visited the Alhambra in the 1840s, declared that the Spaniards actually preferred Charles's palace as 'their building'. It consists of a peristyled courtyard set in the midst of a square building, perhaps modelled on Italian villas though on an uncommonly impressive scale. The rusticated masonry façades of the exterior resemble those found on the exteriors of various Roman and Venetian *palazzi*. On the walls, sculpted medallions celebrate Charles's victories and imperial designs. The rooms inside are larger than those of the Nasrid palaces. Although the columned courtyard in the middle of the palace has a rather austere appearance, Machuca probably planned to create a garden here. Writing of the contrast between the Moorish palaces and the Christian Renaissance palace, the art historian Cammy Brothers declared that 'the Alhambra is additive, multicoloured, sprawling, with internal decoration and outward looking views, while the Christian palace is square, monotone, self-contained, externally ornamented, but inward looking'. There is a long literary tradition disparaging Charles V's palace. In fact it is a fine, imposing building, but on the wrong site.

From the seventeenth century onwards all the palaces of the Alhambra fell upon hard times. There were several earthquakes, as well as fires, both accidental and deliberate. In 1664 the Islamic palaces were designated as an extra-juridical

10. One of the façades of the Palace of Charles V, which was mostly built, though not completed, in the sixteenth century. The rusticated podium of the façade, and indeed the design of the whole palace, is very much in the style that was then fashionable in Italy. Although Charles's palace is an architectural masterpiece in its own right, its scale and its situation cheek-by-jowl with the Nasrid palaces of the Alhambra has been condemned by many as an act of vandalism.

asylum for debtors. At other times the buildings housed galley slaves, invalid soldiers, prisoners, convicts and gypsies, and were also thought to be the ideal place for storing gunpowder. French troops, who occupied the palaces during the Peninsular War, succeeded in blowing up eight of the Moorish towers and the buildings suffered further damage during the Carlist War of 1812. In the early nineteenth century the Patio del Cuarto Dorado was being used as an animal pen and the palaces of the Alhambra had become a kind of agricultural shanty village. According to Richard Ford, the 'uneven weed-encrusted' outer courtyard of the Alhambra was 'disfigured by invalids, beggars and convicts, the outer signs of Spanish weakness and poverty'. In 1870 the buildings were declared a national monument (but even today much of the site is in private hands). Nineteenth-century tourists not only liked to carve their names on the walls, but some of them chiselled out bits of stucco to take away as souvenirs. In 1890 an arsonist started a fire under the north gallery of the Court of Myrtles which did considerable damage.

The historian tends to see the Alhambra as an historical document and, on the whole, that is the point of view that I share. However, that is not the only way of looking at it and the Patronato seems more concerned with catering to the needs and expectations of tourists. Their obedient shuffle in snaking gangs through the palace is evidently very different from the way a medieval Moor entered the place, conducted his business and took his rest there. Even as a tourist oneself, it is hard not to be irritated by one's fellow tourists. Many of them are so wrapped up in what the audio guide or the tour leader is telling them that they seem to find the actual buildings a bit of a distraction. Some amusement can be obtained from dating the various obsolete theories about the buildings that are recycled by so many of the tour guides. According to the Lonely Planet guide to Andalusia, an average of 6,000 tourists a day pass through the Alhambra. Catering to the visitors has certainly distorted the way the Alhambra looks today. On the other hand, the place would not be standing at all if it were not for the money generated by tourists. And at least some of those tourists may become part of the buildings' history too. Washington Irving and Chateaubriand were our predecessors.

2

POISONED PARADISE

In Italy for thirty years under the Borgias they had warfare, terror, murder and bloodshed, but they produced Michelangelo, Leonardo da Vinci and the Renaissance. In Switzerland, they had brotherly love; they had five hundred years of democracy and peace – and what did that produce? The cuckoo clock.

Harry Lime (played by Orson Welles) in *The Third Man*

The Alhambra seems a place of enchantment. Tourism has made it a place of pleasure and instruction. It is easy for those who walk around it today to fantasise about the gilded and cultured existence of the Moors who once inhabited this palace complex – perfumes, prayer and women – a foretaste of paradise. Indeed, James Dickie has written that 'Granada before the fall was a paradise.' Though this must have been true in some respects, in others, Granada in the fourteenth and fifteenth centuries was a special kind of hell and some of the darkest chambers of that hell were to be found inside the Alhambra. The place is a monument to murder, slavery, poverty and fear.

By the fourteenth century slavery had disappeared from most of western Europe, but not from Spain. The palaces of the Alhambra were built upon suffering and the spoils of war.

Christian captives were employed as slave labour in their building. Fourteenth-century verses inscribed on the walls of the Alhambra actually make this boast:

> You imposed chains on the captives and dawn found them
> at your door building your palaces as your servants.

The slaves were probably lodged at night in the prison of the Alcazaba (though there was another prison situated on the main street of the palace complex). The prison was a conically shaped underground chamber in the basement of the Torre de la Vela (the Watch-Tower) at the western end of the Alcazaba and the only access to it would have been by a rope ladder. The dungeon would then be sealed by a trap door, leaving the prisoners with no light and no sanitation. Elsewhere in Granada Christians were employed in plantation slavery.

According to the fourteenth-century historian and philosopher, Ibn Khaldun, the 'Christians pushed the Muslims back to the seacoast and the rugged territory there, where the soil is poor for cultivation of grain and little suited to growing vegetables.' Granada needed to import food from elsewhere, often from its Christian neighbours. It survived politically by paying tribute to Castile and soliciting protection from the Merinid sultans in Morocco. The sultanate's territories were never extensive and its existence was always fraught. The buildings of the Alhambra themselves testify to the poverty of Nasrid rulers, for, though their design and decoration may be magnificent, the materials used are not. As the poet and critic Théophile Gautier observed, the Alhambra was built 'neither in marble nor alabaster, nor even in humble stone'. The palaces are like so many film sets, faking their magnificence in stucco, wood and tiles, and in this respect the Alhambra resembles Mameluke monuments being put up in Cairo in the same century. Michael Rogers, in a study of the *madrasa*, or teaching college, of the Egyptian Sultan al-Zahir Barquq (r. 1382–9, 1390–99) has shown how that superficially magnificent building used sycamore wood as a substitute for bronze. Other precious materials were looted from the buildings of Barquq's predecessors. Since bronze, brass, marble and wood were all in short supply in Egypt, 'the shortage of decorative materials imposed inventiveness in their decoration and use ... Fashion was necessity made a virtue.' Rogers's verdict on the *madrasa* of Barquq can also be applied to the Alhambra.

Critics have noted that both Nasrid art and poetry were deliberately Arab and archaic. Artists and poets looked back to grander times and more opulent palaces that had been lost to the infidel in thirteenth-century Seville and, before that, in eleventh-century Cordoba and they looked back even further to the political and architectural glories of Umayyad Syria and Abbasid Iraq. Scholars in fourteenth- and fifteenth-century Granada were conscious of belonging to a backwoods culture on the perimeter of Islam. The great cultural centres were then in Cairo, Damascus, Samarkand and Herat. The whole of Muslim Andalusian culture was suffused by nostalgia for what could never come again. The Alhambra was an attempt to replicate the glories of previous palaces of vanished dynasties but with only limited resources.

The splendours of the Nasrid palaces pale besides those of their predecessors, the Umayyad caliphs of Cordoba. In the tenth century, when the Umayyad caliphs governed almost all of Spain, they built a palace a few kilometres outside Cordoba called Madinat al-Zahra. It was claimed that 10,000 workmen toiled on this palace. The Byzantine emperor Constantine Porphyrogenitus sent 140 marble columns for its adornment. The Hall of the Caliphs was lined with variously tinted slabs of marble and at its centre was a pool of mercury which caught the sunlight and which could be stirred so as to send dazzling flashes of sunlight round the room. The ponds of the palace needed 12,000 loaves of bread a day to keep the fishes fed. But the Umayyad caliphate was a provincial backwater by comparison with the Abbasid caliphate in the East and the splendours of Madinat al-Zahra could not match those of the Abbasid palaces in Baghdad and Samarra. When a Byzantine delegation arrived in Baghdad in 917, they were taken around one of the many palaces of the caliph. According to al-Khatib's *History of Baghdad*:

> Now there were no soldiers here, but only the eunuchs and the chamberlains and the black pages. The number of the eunuchs was seven thousand in all; the number of the chamberlains was also seven thousand, and the number of the black pages, other than the eunuchs, was four thousand; the flat roofs of the palaces being occupied by them, as also of the banqueting halls. Further, the store-chambers had been opened, and the treasures therein set out as is customary for a bride's array; the jewels of the caliph being arranged in trays, on steps, and covered with cloths of black brocade. When the ambassadors entered the Palace of the Tree, their astonishment was great. For there they saw birds fashioned out of silver and whistling with every motion, while perched on a tree of silver weighing 500 dirhams …

The ambassadors were also shown the gold brocade hangings, the carpets, the richly harnessed horses, the Park of Wild Beasts, the elephants caparisoned in peacock-silk brocade, the lions in chains, the lake of tin on which floated pleasure boats covered in gold embroideries, the tree with gold and silver branches and much else besides before being finally ushered into the throne room of the caliph. The string of Abbasid palaces in ninth-century Samarra spread out along the Tigris were ornamented with glass mosaic, marble, lustre ceramics, lapis lazuli, ivory and ebony. By comparison with the palaces of the caliphs, the Alhambra was a shadow of a shadow. (And looking further ahead, it must be apparent that the palaces of Saddam Hussein in Iraq owe more to American motels than they do to anything in the Islamic tradition.)

RED DEATHS OF THE SULTANS

A dispassionate scrutiny of the history of the Nasrid sultans of Granada reveals that they presided precariously over a poisoned paradise. Antonio Fernández-Puertas has pointed out that of the first nine sultans, from Muhammad I to Ismail II (1232–1360), one died in an accident, one was deposed and thereafter died a natural death, and the remaining seven were assassinated. As we shall see, the life expectancy of the ministers of the Nasrid sultans was no better either. Red Death stalked the corridors of the Alhambra. (*Mawt al-Alhmar*, or Red Death, means violent death, whereas White Death referred to dying peacefully in one's sleep.) In Nasrid Spain and in contemporaneous Merinid Morocco, violence was the chief engine of politics.

Arabs and Berbers had first entered Spain in 711. For several centuries their control over almost all the peninsula, except for Galicia, was uncontested. But in 1031 the caliphate of Cordoba fell apart, the victim of military feuds. Thereafter the Muslim territory in Spain was divided up among the petty regimes of the Muluk al-Tawa'if, or Party Kings, and increasingly threatened by the gathering pace of the Christian *Reconquista*. In order to defend themselves from the Christians, the Party Kings had recourse first, in the eleventh and twelfth centuries, to the Almoravids, a North African Berber dynasty, and later, in the twelfth and thirteenth centuries, to the Almohads, a similar dynasty (though of a more puritanical and intolerant disposition). In the early thirteenth century the Almohad power base in North Africa was being challenged by rival Berber clans and they withdrew from Spain, leaving the Muslims to face the *Reconquista* alone. Cordoba was captured by the Christians in 1236 and Seville in 1248. The Nasrid sultanate of Granada was founded in 1232 by Muhammad I al-Ghalib, also called Ibn al-Ahmar. A pious leader of a small war band who took over after the withdrawal of the Almohads, he struggled with limited success to defend the territory he had usurped from Christian Castile.

Muhammad I (who extended and rebuilt the Alcazaba) died after a fall from his horse in 1273. Muhammad II, who had to defend his territories not just from the Castilians, but also from a rebel Arab tribe called the Banu Ashqilula, died in 1302. According to Ibn al-Khatib (on whom more below), the sultan was poisoned by his own son, who fed him a ring of poisoned batter. The son, Muhammad III, was a refined poet, sadist and enthusiast for architecture. (He built the mosque of the Alhambra.) When he heard that a jailer had shown pity to some slaves who were being starved to death in one of the dungeons of the palace, he had that jailer beheaded in such a manner that his head and blood fell upon the slaves. When he became blind he ruled through his vizier, but in 1309 the vizier was murdered by a rival and Muhammad III was thereupon forced to abdicate. His brother Nasr succeeded him. When Nasr had a stroke Muhammad attempted to retake the throne, but Nasr recovered and had his brother imprisoned. Not long afterwards Muhammad's corpse was found floating in one of the pools of the palace.

Nasr was an expert in mathematics and astronomy but not in politics and he was in turn forced to abdicate in 1314. A cousin, Ismail, succeeded and held power until in 1325 he was stabbed to death by a cousin in a quarrel over a slave girl. (It was Ismail I who founded the Mexuar, though it would be hard to say how much of the building that stands today is his work. Similarly, he built the first version of the Comares Palace, though hardly any of his work survived the rebuilding by his successors. The Generalife also probably dates back to his reign.) Ismail's son and successor, Muhammad IV, was put on the throne at the age of nine. After the assassination of his vizier, Ibn al-Mahruq, in 1328 or 1329, he was effectively prisoner and puppet of the clan of the Bani Abi'l-'Ula. Muhammad busied himself with his horses. The great famine occurred in 1329 and for years afterwards the peasantry of Granada struggled to live on stores of mouldy grain. Because of continuing threats from Castile and loss of territory to the Christians, Muhammad IV became heavily dependent on assistance from the Merinids, and he was murdered in 1333 by the Bani Abi'l-'Ula, because they thought that the ruler's relations with the Merinids were too close. Obviously it would be a mistake to think of the Nasrid sultanate as an unfettered despotism. Not only was that despotism tempered by assassination, but, even when the reigning sultan was not being directly menaced by the knife, he was often not so much ruling as holding the ring for over-mighty and contending Arab or Berber clans.

Muhammad IV was succeeded by his brother Yusuf, who was only fifteen at the time of his accession. Ibn al-Khatib observed that at first the young sultan's royal writ ran no further than the power to decide what he would have for dinner. It was during Yusuf I's reign (1333–54) that a joint army of Nasrids and Merinids was defeated by the armies of Castile, Aragon and Portugal at the Battle of Rio Salado in 1340. The Merinid forces then withdrew from Andalusia and this marked the end of any effective military assistance for Granada from North Africa. It was also during the reign of Yusuf I that the Black Death raged through Granada from 1348 onwards. It particularly affected slum-dwellers and undernourished peasants. There were rumours that many Muslims were thinking of converting to Christianity in the hope that this offered some form of medical protection. Despite this sombre backdrop, Yusuf I, who, like his successor Muhammad V, was allegedly fascinated by architecture, oversaw much of the building of the Comares Palace (in particular the Hall of the Ambassadors), as well as the Tower of the Captive, and founded a *madrasa* in Granada. The poets Ibn al-Jayyab and Ibn al-Khatib entered the sultan's service and were successively his viziers. Yusuf was stabbed to death in 1354 by a mad black slave in the great Mosque of Granada.

Although Yusuf had favoured his younger son, Ismail, the senior statesmen, Ridwan and Ibn al-Khatib, put the older son, Muhammad on the throne. Muhammad V (1354–9 and 1362–91) was sixteen at the time he first came to the throne and affairs were run by his ministers. He depended for his security on a Christian bodyguard, but they could not save him from being deposed by his half-brother, Ismail, in 1359. Muhammad's chamberlain, Ridwan, was murdered and Muhammad V and his partisans went into exile in Merinid Fez. (As we shall see, that sojourn in Morocco had a considerable influence both on the later politicking in Granada and on the architecture and decoration of the Court of the Lions.) The corpulent and effeminate Ismail II was murdered in 1360 by his cousin Abu 'Abd Allah Muhammad, a loutish hashish addict afflicted by nervous tics, who became Muhammad VI. In 1362 Muhammad V returned from exile in Fez and, with the support of Pedro the Cruel (r. 1350–69), the King of Castile, regained his throne and Pedro personally killed Muhammad VI with a lance. Like Yusuf I before him, Muhammad V benefited from a close alliance with the King of Castile. (Pedro the Cruel was so called because of his penchant for murder. In the context of fourteenth-century Spanish politics, it was quite something to be awarded the sobriquet 'Cruel'.)

Pedro was an enthusiast for Muslim culture and imported craftsmen from Granada to work on the Alcazar of Seville (1364 onwards). This palace, and especially its Salón de Ambajadores, with its combination of a tiled dado and intricate stucco above, is reminiscent of the Alhambra. One even finds the Muslim and Nasrid motto *La ghalib ila Allah* ('No victor but God') on tiles on the walls of this Christian palace.

Doubtless both owe something to the Merinid palace in Fez which no longer exists in its medieval form. Pedro was killed in 1369 after being defeated at the Battle of Montiel by his stepbrother Henry, and with Pedro's death the close alliance of Granada and Castile came to an end. (So too did Muhammad V's building work on the Alhambra.) Although Muhammad V had been an ally of the King of Castile, the chaos of Pedro's assassination allowed him to repossess Algeciras in July 1369 – an event that some scholars think the Court of the Lions was built to commemorate. Certainly the Comares Palace, and especially its façade, was completed in 1370 and it is very likely that building work was financed by loot from the Algeciras campaign. However, there is no direct evidence for the Court of the Lions being some sort of victory monument and on chronological grounds it seems unlikely. Apart from completing the Comares Palace and building the Court of the Lions, Muhammad V also rebuilt the Mexuar area. Yusuf I and Muhammad V were the sultans chiefly responsible for the Alhambra as we see it today. They have come down in history as capable, cultured and popular rulers and they very well may have been just that. However, these favourable portraits are based overwhelmingly on the testimony of their functionary and panegyrist Ibn al-Khatib and it is very hard to see behind that testimony.

There are no good Arabic sources for events in Granada after the death of Muhammad V and throughout the fifteenth century. The lack of such sources may suggest the place had become an intellectual backwater. It is indeed remarkable that we are better informed about the history of Cordoba under the Umayyads in the tenth and eleventh centuries than we are about the history of Granada in the late

Middle Ages. Muhammad V's successor, Yusuf II (1391–2), was at first the puppet of a servant of his father, Khalid, who murdered three of the sultan's brothers, before the sultan succeeded in murdering him. Yusuf II died of poison (allegedly it was his robe that was coated with poison), but we are poorly informed about his successors and even the dates of their reigns are conjectural.

After the death of Muhammad V, there was hardly any building work carried out within the precincts of the Alhambra. Muhammad VII (1392–1408) built the Tower of the Princesses, though the scholarly consensus is that the building's design and ornamentation show clear evidence of the decline of craftsmanship. Periods of internal turmoil alternated or sometimes overlapped with periods of warfare with Christian neighbours. One particular internal feud is worth dwelling on. This was the rivalry between a powerful clan known as the Banu Sarraj and their enemies. In 1419 they deposed Muhammad VIII and put Muhammad IX on the throne. Although Muhammad IX, a violent and not terribly popular ruler, was deposed several times, the Banu Sarraj remained a power in the land. Muhammad IX was succeeded by Muhammad XI in 1451. (Muhammad X had been one of those ill-fated would-be rulers put on the throne during one of the periods in which Muhammad IX was deposed.) Muhammad XI had his throat slit and his children were suffocated by Abu Nasr Sa'd, who then usurped the sultanate. According to legend, the new sultan invited the Banu Sarraj to dinner in the Alhambra and had most of them massacred. In fact he seems to have been successful in murdering only a couple of the Banu Sarraj, but chroniclers and poets in the nineteenth century commemorated this as the notorious slaughter of the Abencerrages and guides took to pointing out to tourists the red stain in the marble of the fountain in the Hall of the Abencerrages as evidence of the atrocity that had taken place there.

The last decades of the sultanate of Granada are a story of diminishing options. Despite the external threat from the Christian kingdoms, internal struggles for control of the shrinking territory continued unabated. The last sultan, Muhammad XII, better known to later writers in the West as Boabdil, having deposed his father in a palace coup, reigned intermittently from 1482 until 1492 in competition with various of his kinsmen. In 1479 Aragon and Castile were united through the marriage of Ferdinand and Isabella. In 1485 Boabdil recognised Ferdinand of Castile's overlordship of the province of Granada, but the Christians continued to occupy ever more of the sultanate and by 1489 only the town of Granada and the Alhambra remained in Muslim hands. Granada was starved into submission, and on 2 January 1492, in the Hall of the Ambassadors, Boabdil surrendered the keys of the city to the Spaniards. The Castilian flag was then raised over the watch-tower of the Alcazaba. *La ghalib ila Allah.*

In the 1930s the historian and biographer Philip Guedalla wrote a beguiling counter-factual essay entitled 'If the Moors in Spain Had Won …' After outlining the decisive defeat of the Catholic kings at the Battle of Lanjaron in 1491 and their abandonment of any hope of capturing Granada, he went on to consider the consequences for Europe of the survival of a Moorish kingdom into modern times. He also provided his readers with the relevant section from Baedeker's guide to *North Africa and the Barbary Coast, including the Kingdom of*

Granada. In Guedalla's guidebook fantasy, Granada in the early twentieth century is the capital of King Boabdil V and the residence of a Grand Mufti. As for the Alhambra, this

> contains the Royal Palace, the great proportion of the
> Government buildings (Ministries of War, Marine, Foreign
> Affairs and Wakfs), and a handsome War Memorial. The Great
> Mosque (Djamia el-Kebîr), venerated throughout Islam under
> the name of 'Mosque of the Spur' from the spurs discarded by
> King Ferdinand in his precipitate flight from the Battlefield of
> Lanjaron ...

The Palais Royal de l'Alhambra is a two-star tourist attraction, 'accessible in the absence of the royal family by written permission from the Ministry of the Interior. The private apartments are not shown.' Visitors to the Generalife are warned to be careful 'as the royal menagerie is situated here'. Counter-factual or 'What if?' history is fun and one may speculate, as Guedalla implicitly did, about the loss to European culture and science occasioned by the historical fall of Granada and the expulsion of the Moors from Spain. However, as W. H. Auden wrote in his poem 'Spain 1937':

> History to the defeated
> May say Alas but cannot help or pardon.

RED DEATHS OF THE VIZIERS

If it was dangerous to be a king, it was no less dangerous to be the king's chief minister, for it was usual for a vizier's career to be ended by his murder. There is no need to chronicle the unhappy ends of all of them here, but two ministers in particular, Ibn al-Khatib and Ibn Zamrak, were associated with the design and decoration of the Alhambra. Yusuf I's vizier and court poet, 'Ali ibn al-Jayyab, was carried off by the Black Death in 1349. Ibn al-Khatib, who succeeded him as vizier, actually wrote a treatise on the plague in which he unorthodoxly argued that the pestilence was spread by contagion. (The Prophet Muhammad had denied that it was possible for the plague to be spread in that way.)

Lisan al-Din ibn al-Khatib (1313–75) was born in a village outside Granada and came from a line of nobly born bureaucrats. Ibn al-Jayyab was one of his early teachers and when he became vizier he extended his patronage to Ibn al-Khatib and made him his personal secretary. Ibn al-Khatib was an eloquent writer, as the first part of his name, Lisan al-Din (Tongue of the Faith) testifies. Having become vizier of Sultan Yusuf I, Ibn al-Khatib retained that office under Muhammad V and, when Muhammad was deposed in 1359, he accompanied him into exile in North Africa before returning to power with him in 1362. On his return to office in Granada, Ibn al-Khatib pursued a series of vendettas against his rivals and seems to have forged incriminating correspondence in furtherance of that aim. The political and cultural contacts he had made during the years of exile in the Merinid sultanate from 1359 to 1362, strongly influenced his thinking, and there are grounds for supposing that what he and his sovereign saw in Morocco was the main influence on the building work carried on in the Alhambra in the years immediately after the return from exile. Throughout his political career Ibn al-Khatib remained a strong advocate of the importance of the Merinid alliance for resisting the *Reconquista*. His book *The Shaking of the Bag. On the Diversion of One Who Travels* was chiefly devoted to describing the Merinid lands.

During his exile Ibn al-Khatib seems to have spent most of his time at Salé (close to Rabat on the Atlantic coast) and there he immersed himself in the study of Sufism and mystical meditation. This was a period when the popularity and influence of Sufism was spreading throughout North Africa and Spain. (The fourteenth-century traveller Ibn Battuta noted that a number of Persian and Indian Sufis had chosen to settle in Granada and he also visited several *zawiya*s or Sufi convents there.) The famous North African writer, politician and mystic Muhammad ibn Ahmad ibn Marzuq (1310–79) was one of Ibn al-Khatib's Sufi teachers. Ibn al-Khatib also made a close study of the writings of the great thirteenth-century Andalusian Sufi Muhyi al-Din ibn 'Arabi. Ibn 'Arabi was the towering presence in late medieval Islamic mysticism. All men of education read him, though some suspected his orthodoxy. His metaphysics was strongly influenced by the Neoplatonism of the Brethren of Purity (on which, see the next chapter). For Ibn 'Arabi, beauty was a manifestation of God. Ibn al-Khatib set out his own mystical ideas in *Rawdat al-ta'rif bi al-hubb al-sharif* ('The Garden of Instruction in Noble Love'), where he wrote of divine love and the growth of its allegorical tree and advocated constant practice of *dhikr* (remembrance of God) and contemplation of divine beauty. He believed that it was literally true that love made the world go round. However, despite his mystical tendencies, he was notoriously fond of luxury. In his palace he had a glass pavilion with a water cascade. (One of the

Seljuk sultans in Anatolia also had a glass palace. It is not surprising that neither of these edifices, nor the Ghaznavid pavilion made of halva, has survived.)

He was a prolific author and his books included works on travel, medicine, poetry, political theory, history and biographical dictionaries. He wrote a treatise on princes who came to the throne before reaching the age of majority. He produced two anthologies of chancery documents that he had drafted. He wrote an essay on travelling in summer and winter. He composed many *muwashshah*s. (The *muwashshah* was a five- to seven-stanza verse form intended for musical recitation. Most commonly this genre of poetry commemorated hopeless love and the cruelty of the beloved. Though the matter remains controversial, many Arabists argue that the *muwashshah* exercised a decisive influence on the Provençal troubador lyric.) This was an age when poetry was an instrument of politics and the most common vehicle for political propaganda. All major state occasions were marked by flatulently pompous odes. Ibn al-Khatib's industry as a scholar, poet and statesman (an industry that was facilitated by chronic insomnia) led his contemporaries to refer to him as *Dhu al-'Umrayn*, 'the Man of Two Lives'. That he slept badly is hardly surprising, as politics at the Nasrid court was a dangerous business and Ibn al-Khatib had made many enemies. Towards the end of his career he was driven to revise his biographical dictionary, *Al-Katiba al-Kamina*, 'Troops in Ambush', because so many of his friends who had featured in it had turned into enemies. He believed that, in the long run, all regimes and dynasties were doomed by the corruption, ambition and greed of those who served them. He had an aristocratic contempt for the fickle and vulgar masses – 'deaf, dumb and mindless'. 'The Sallust of the Kingdom of Granada' saw history as a vicious cycle of usurpations and depositions. The philosopher-historian Ibn Khaldun shared this gloomy view of the political process. The two writer-statesmen maintained a fraught and intermittent friendship. Though Ibn Khaldun is more widely read today (for his ideas about the cyclical fall of dynasties and the sociology of Islam, among other things), Ibn al-Khatib was in his day the grander figure and a more stylish writer.

The reason why we know so much about Ibn al-Khatib is that, about two hundred years later, a North African scholar, al-Maqqari (c. 1577–1632), wrote an enormous history of Muslim Spain and a biography of its most famous vizier, *Nafh al-Tibb min Ghusn al-Andalus al-Ratib wa-Dhikr Waziriha Lisan al-Din ibn al-Khatib*, ('The Fragrant Scent of the Tender Shoots of Andalus and the History of the Vizier Lisan al-Din ibn al-Khatib'). Al-Maqqari, who was resident in Damascus at the time, wrote a book that was suffused with romantic nostalgia for an Andalus that was lost to the Muslims for ever. Ibn al-Khatib was his hero. However, the twentieth-century scholar Emilio García Gómez drew upon the material provided by al-Maqqari and others to present quite a different portrait. He argued that Ibn al-Khatib was ambitious and greedy. His numerous literary works, though prolific and wide-ranging, were marred by wilfully obscure vocabulary and constructions. García Gómez's Ibn al-Khatib was a gloomy and neurotic figure, haunted by his awareness that the days of the Muslims in Spain were numbered and drawn to mysticism by a fear of death.

Ibn al-Khatib's consistently pro-Merinid policy and his insistence on the need for Moroccan support in order to resist Christian encroachments was unpopular with a lot of his fellow courtiers and it was probably the steep decline in the military and political power of the Merinids that sealed his fate. Rumours circulated that he was plotting with the Merinid sultan, 'Abd al-'Aziz, against Muhammad V. It seems likely that some of those rumours were put about by Ibn al-Khatib's deputy, Ibn Zamrak. In 1371 Ibn al-Khatib fled to Morocco, where he was safe for a while, as 'Abd al-'Aziz protected him, but the sultan died in 1372 and his successor, Muhammad III, was vulnerable to political pressure from Nasrid Granada. Ibn al-Khatib was arrested and, although the reasons for wanting him dead were political, he faced trumped-up charges of heresy. His enemies combed his mystical treatise for evidence that he espoused both an atheistic form of *falasafa* (philosophy) and *hulul* (incarnationism, that is, the doctrine that God is present in the world). Awaiting death in prison in Fez, he wrote poetry, including the lines: 'We used to feed others, but lo, now we are food for worms.' His trial never came to a conclusion but he was strangled anyway by a special execution squad from Granada headed by Ibn Zamrak. Later Ibn al-Khatib's corpse was disinterred to be burnt by his enemies. So it was remarked that he ended up as 'the man of two deaths'.

The man who had overseen the judicial murder of Ibn al-Khatib was also a man of high culture. Abu 'Abdallah Muhammad ibn Yusuf ibn Zamrak (d. after 1393) was the son of a smith (whom, it is alleged, he eventually murdered with a blow to the head). Ibn Zamrak owed his advancement to the patronage of Ibn al-Khatib, who was one of his teachers at the newly founded *madrasa* in Granada. Ibn Zamrak was obviously bright and he became Ibn al-Khatib's secretary and wrote panegyrics about him. Like Ibn al-Khatib, Ibn Zamrak followed Muhammad V into exile in North Africa, where he studied Sufism with Ibn Marzuq. On return to Spain, in 1362 Ibn Zamrak was made Muhammad's private secretary, with the special job of composing *qasidas* (odes) to commemorate public events. He wrote sixty-six, of which about twenty survive. He wrote descriptive poetry in the manner of the twelfth-century Andalusian poet Ibn Khafaja – that is to say he specialised in evocations of nature, gardens and the pleasures of life. (*Nawriyyat*, flower poetry, and *rawdiyyat*, garden poetry, were recognised genres of Arabic literature.) Inevitably Ibn Zamrak wrote about the Alhambra and its gardens. His *qasida* on the palace garden and astronomy works with entirely traditional themes and is indeed a celebration of artifice. The poem praises artifice at the expense of nature, the palace at the expense of the garden (and there is also a hint that his poetry is better than either). He worked with utterly conventional metaphors. For example, pearls are equivalent to verses and verses are equivalent to stars. The glorious Alhambra is a metonym for Muhammad V and so forth. Ibn Zamrak also wrote platitudinous religious poetry. Though his descriptive stuff is better, even so, modern readers are likely to find him mannered and wearisome. Panegyric poetry in any language does not wear well.

Ibn Zamrak seems to have fallen out with Ibn al-Khatib around 1369. Once Ibn al-Khatib fled to Morocco, Ibn Zamrak replaced him as vizier and thereafter he was in and out of office under Muhammad V's successor, Yusuf II. Ibn Zamrak also served Muhammad VII as vizier before being assassinated on that sultan's orders. The murderers found Ibn

Zamrak at home reading the Koran and slaughtered him and his two sons in front of his wives and daughters. Like Ibn al-Khatib, Ibn Zamrak was much later the victim of a hostile study by García Gómez ('Ibn Zamrak, el poeta de la Alhambra').

These two poet-statesmen had a crucial role in planning and overseeing the building of the Court of the Lions and other parts of the Alhambra. Ibn al-Khatib's poem on the party to mark the Prophet's birthday in 1362 is very nearly the only literary source we have on the appearance of the Alhambra prior to 1492. Moreover, their poetry is not just to be found in manuscripts; it also decorates the walls of the Alhambra. The Alhambra is probably the most famous of all the Islamic buildings that provide their own written commentary. It is a text-laden building, an inhabitable book. A literate courtier walking through the palace would learn from one of its towers that 'Nothing can match this work,' while the boast of the Fountain of the Court of the Lions was 'Incomparable is this basin. Allah the exalted one desired that it should surpass everything in wonderful beauty.' Gates and doors within the pavilions instructed readers on their functions. The poetry by Ibn al-Khatib and Ibn Zamrak was often placed at a quite low level. Texts from the Koran, on the other hand, were skied, that is placed at such a height that it was hard for anyone but Allah to read them. In particular, a significant part of a lengthy *qasida* by Ibn Zamrak adorns the walls of the Sala de las Dos Hermanas (Hall of the Two Sisters).

The early nineteenth-century travel writer Richard Ford described the Court of the Lions as 'a Moorish cloister, but one never framed for ascetics'. But appearances notwithstanding, the Court of Lions may indeed have been a place where medieval Muslims studied, prayed and schooled themselves in austerity – precisely a gorgeous frame for religious asceticism. The intellectual and the literary climate of the Nasrid court in the mid-fourteenth century, as well as the North African sojourn of the sultan and his ministers from 1359 to 1362, may well have played crucial roles in determining the function and appearance of the Court of the Lions. It has recently been argued by Juan Carlos Ruiz Souza that the Court of the Lions was not a palace at all, but a *madrasa*. The Court of the Lions then would have lodged scholars who studied the Koran, *hadiths* (sayings of the Prophet), theology and religious law and perhaps also have served as the forum for scholarly debates conducted in front of the sultan. (Ibn Battuta, who was in Fez in 1349, describes the Merinid sultan as holding scholarly assemblies every day after the dawn prayer in the main mosque.) Although from the eleventh century onwards *madrasa*s spread throughout the Islamic world, they were almost unknown in North Africa and Muslim Spain – until, that is, the late thirteenth century. The Merinid sultans were enthusiastic patrons of *madrasa*s and several now-famous ones were commissioned by them in the fourteenth century.

In North Africa the Merinid sultans may have used the *madrasa* as an instrument of patronage to provide a pool of administrators, as well as to weaken any religiously based opposition. It would also have given advanced teaching in

Arabic to students coming in from the countryside, who would most likely have been Berber speakers. The building of *madrasa*s was also, perhaps, a way of buying God's favour. As Tim Mackintosh-Smith has noted in his splendid travelogue *Travels with a Tangerine*, sensible Mameluke sultans of Egypt, bearing in mind the insecurity of their tenure of the throne, 'hurried to build their tombs as soon as possible, and always added a *madrasah*, both to the greater glory of God and as a sort of pension plan for the afterlife'. The same was true of rulers elsewhere in the Islamic world.

The typical Moroccan *madrasa* was usually quite small and was built round a central patio paved in marble or tiled and overlooked by galleries. It usually had a fountain or pool at its centre. The upper storeys of the galleries contained cell-like rooms for the accommodation of students and teachers. What is unusual about Moroccan *madrasa*s, as compared to their Eastern counterparts, is their elaborate decoration, which gives them a rather secular look. Lucien Golvin in his *La Madrasa médiévale* (1995) described the typical Merinid *madrasa* as '*l'Alhambra revue et interprété*'. However, it is obvious from the chronology of the building work and the way the cultural contacts took place that the reverse is true, for it is the Alhambra's Court of the Lions that has to be seen as an imitation and interpretation of the Merinid *madrasa*. The ground floors of the Moroccan *madrasa* commonly have intricate decorative schemes in wood, stucco and tile, whereas the upper-storey cells are bare of decoration (as in the Court of the Lions).

In addition to *madrasa*s, the Merinids also commissioned the building of *zawiya*s. A *zawiya* was a place for Sufis to lodge, study and meditate. In many cases, the syllabus of the *zawiya* overlapped with that of the *madrasa*, and sometimes a building was shared between the Sufis and the other scholars. The *zawiya*s were also richly decorated and there were no significant architectural differences between the two types of building.

As noted, the Moroccan *madrasa*s were usually quite small buildings. The Bu-'Inaniyya *madrasa* (1350–55) in Fez was exceptional in its size. The grandest and last of the Merinid *madrasa*s, it was built round a marble-paved court-yard with a fountain at its centre. The surrounding walls and porticos were densely and intricately decorated with sculpted stucco and tiles. The ceilings were of cedar wood with elaborate *muqarnas* vaulting. The Madrasa Dar al-Majzan, which was situated next to the Merinid palace and whose chief role was to train palace functionaries, was, if anything, even more richly decorated. However, the most striking prototype for the Court of the Lions is to be found in Salé, the main port of Merinid Morocco. Here an inscription in the small but exuberantly decorated *madrasa* founded by Abu'l-Hasan in 1333 (with which Ibn al-Khatib would certainly have been very familiar) makes the following boast: 'Look at my wonderful door! Rejoice at how carefully I am put together, at the remarkable nature of my construction and at my marvellous interior! The craftsmen have completed there a piece of artistic workmanship which has the beauty of youth ...' According to other inscriptions, 'The wonders of this *madrasa* perturb the faculty of reason and captivate both ascetics and the pious alike' and 'I am constructed like a tiered palace and sparkle like rows of pearls on the neck of one that is engaged to be married.' These sorts of inscription closely parallel those composed by Ibn al-Khatib and Ibn

11. A *madrasa*, or religious teaching college at Salé in Morocco (built in 1333). The intimacy of its scale and extravagant decoration anticipates those features in the Alhambra's Court of the Lions. It is unlikely to be a coincidence that the vizier Ibn al-Khatib, who must have been closely involved with the building of the Court of the Lions, spent most of his years in exile in Salé.

Zamrak for the Alhambra, and the decor͟...
courtyard of the Salé *madrasa* parallels that ͟...
the Lions. In *Travels with a Tangerine* Macki͟...
describes it as follows:

> *Crossing the threshold into its courtyard was like opening a plai͟...*
> *cloth binding to find it contains a pop-up book vividly coloured*
> *in greengage-green, sky blue, royal blue, turquoise, ivory and*
> *cinnamon … Every single surface was covered either in carving*
> *or in polychrome tilework, as if the designer had suffered from*
> *acute* horror vacui. *The overall effect was of a very expensive*
> *bibelot.*

The similarity of the filigree stucco work at the Salé *madrasa* to that in the Alhambra is striking and suggests the possibility of a common pool of artisans. Golvin, who is not so fond of the intricate stucco work and elaborate *muqarnas* work of these *madrasa*s, has declared that '*cette sorte de débauche aux XIIIe et XIVe siècles se situe bien dans la note du temps et l'Alhambre de Grenade, dans les chambres qui entourent la fameuse Cour des Lions, en faisant également un veritable abus au XIVe siècle*'.

The first *madrasa* in the town of Granada was built in 1349, as an inscription preserved on marble tablets, now in the Alhambra Museum, testifies. The North African Sufi Ibn Marzuq came over to lecture there in 1353 and Ibn Zamrak studied there. (Although this building was mostly demolished in the early eighteenth century, it is clear that it was modelled on the Merinid *madrasa*s of North Africa.) It would have been a little odd if the palace-city of the Alhambra did not also have its own *madrasa*. Souza suggests

12. The Court of the Lions looking westwards. The dome added by Contreras to the pavilion on the other side has vanished, but the slope of the restored roof is still at too steep an angle. Watercourses and fountains in the courtyard and the surrounding buildings have the effect of eliding the distinction between interior and exterior.

that the Court of the Lions is located precisely where one would expect the *madrasa* to be, as it occupies a zone of transition between the Comares Palace and the Rawda, or garden-cemetery. The palace *madrasa*, if that indeed is what it was, would also have contained the royal library and probably the books would have been stored in alcove cupboards in the Sala de los Reyes. (In the medieval Islamic world it was not customary to shelve books; rather they were piled side-down in cupboards or store chests.) The ceiling frescos then can be read as showing scholars and different genres of literature. The Nasrid library was, like so many Muslim libraries, presumably destroyed by Cardinal Cisneros, who regarded all Arabic books as manuals of infidelity and sorcery. After he became Archbishop of Granada in 1499, he organised a vast bonfire of Arabic manuscripts in the main square of the city.

Within the *madrasa* of the Court of the Lions, the Hall of the Abencerrages would have been the oratory, or prayer room. The hypothesis that this chamber had a religious function is supported by the fact that there are no secular poems by Ibn Zamrak or anyone else here. The only inscriptions are Koranic ones. However, if it was a prayer room, it is curious that there is no sign of a *mihrab* (prayer niche indicating the direction of worship). But then again, it is worth bearing in mind that the Great Mosque of the Alhambra was only just across the street. Incidentally, it was a common feature of Moroccan mosques that they also functioned as places of instruction and it was common for *madrasa*s to be built next to mosques, so that teachers and students could easily pass from one to the other. The Patio of the Harem just to the west of the Hall of the Abencerrages on the south side of the courtyard was probably where the *muqaddam* (overseer) of

13. The famous Vase of the Gazelles (now in the Museum of the Alhambra) is one of a group of broadly similar Alhambra Vases. Its glazed and painted earthenware has been painted with cobalt and lustre. Since it is 135cm high, it is effectively a ceramic sculpture and, as such, it and similar vases were used to decorate the palaces of the Alhambra.

the *madrasa* had his office. So perhaps we should dismiss from our imaginings voluptuous, houri-eyed singing girls reclining on carpets and substitute in their place a grizzled janitor doling out pious texts and loaves of unleavened bread to the young male students in his charge. The Court of the Lions would have served as a place of scholarship and prayer. It would have trained bureaucrats to serve the sultan as well as pious and erudite conversationalists to edify him. Like the men and women who endowed chantry chapels in medieval England, pious Muslims who established *madrasa*s often did so in the hope that this virtuous act would ensure their soul's salvation. Reasoning by analogy with Moroccan examples, Souza believes that Muhammad V's tomb may have been located within the Hall of the Abencerrages. To sum up, it seems most probable, though not certain, that the Court of the Lions was no palace, but a religious teaching college. Whether it was or not, it certainly belonged in the same architectural tradition as that of the Muslim teaching college, for its close resemblance to the *madrasa*s of Merinid Morocco is unmistakable. Had Charles V not destroyed the façade of this complex, there would be no need for argument as there would certainly have been a foundation inscription placed above or beside the entrance.

The Alhambra was a place designed by poets and inhabited by scholars. Many of these poets and scholars came to tragic ends. Ibn al-Khatib and Ibn Zamrak did not find paradise in this world. It is time now to consider in more detail the visual fruits of their scholarly deliberations and mystical meditations.

3

A PALACE TO THINK IN

The dimensions of this pavilion, its adjacent rooms, the approaches, the galleries surrounding it, the gardens, the many pools and fountains, the walks, and the steps and levels – every one exactly specified, prescribed, measured, and in the damnedest of measurements – everything in halves and quarters and bits and pieces, irregularities and unexpectedness.

Doris Lessing, *The Marriage Between Zones Three, Four and Five*
(London, 1980)

It is strange that the building should give so much pleasure to today's profane hordes of infidel visitors for whom it emphatically was not built. The Alhambra was designed by and for intellectuals with mystical inclinations. It was a machine for thinking in. Its lacework decoration and watery reflections hint at the impermanence of all material and visible things. The beauty of the Alhambra is based upon proportion and upon abstract geometric designs of staggering complexity. What did the educated medieval Arab see when he gazed on those patterns? Was the place merely 'a museum of geometrical shapes', as Oleg Grabar has put it (and, indeed, as Owen Jones treated it), or were the complex structures of the Alhambra underpinned by a geometry that had mystical resonance?

The sense of harmony experienced when walking around the buildings suggests that the place was designed according to certain mathematical principles. My own view is that the set-piece parts of the Alhambra were designed and built under the direction of Ibn al-Khatib and other intellectuals and mystics, and that is what will be argued later in this chapter. However, it must be conceded in advance that there is little direct evidence for this and an alternative way of thinking about the building is worth considering, however briefly. In the medieval Islamic world, buildings were not credited to architects. If anyone got the credit, it was the ruler who commissioned the building. Being an architect was not an identifiable profession. A person who designed a building might be referred to as a *muhandis*, but the primary meaning of this word was 'geometer' and it might also be used of an engineer or surveyor. Stresses and loads were not calculated, as the mathematics for doing this had not yet been developed. Masons relied on past experience and, if there was any doubt about the stresses, they tended to overcompensate, for instance, by building the walls extra thick. Even so, there were often accidents and the history of Islamic architecture is littered with collapsed domes and fallen minarets. There were no technical manuals on architecture and architectural techniques were transmitted orally.

Most buildings in the Islamic world seem to have been put up by mostly illiterate artisans according to empirical techniques and without any preliminary ground plan on paper. Jonathan Bloom in a recent, ground-breaking book on the history of paper in the Islamic world, comments as follows: 'Literate people today tend to forget that the ability to conceptualize and represent three-dimensional spaces on

two-dimensional surfaces (and decode these representations) is an extremely sophisticated skill, one that has been honed in the West since the Renaissance.' And Bloom cites an encounter between Arthur Upham Pope, a well-known twentieth-century expert on Persian art, and a master mason from Isfahan. Pope asked the mason about the details of building a brick squinch:

> *He seemed stumped. So I handed him a sheet of paper and a pencil. He held them at arm's length, a look of total hopelessness on his ... face ... He was illiterate: more, he was incapable of presenting a three-dimensional object in two flat dimensions. He put the pencil aside, then folded the paper intricately to construct an actual squinch.*

Certainly one should not underestimate the technical ingenuity of illiterate artisans. However, there are indications that highly literate intellectuals dictated the design of the Alhambra and determined its proportions. As has been noted, significant areas of the wall surfaces are decorated with calligraphy and much of this consisted of extracts from poems by officials who served the sultan as vizier or head of the chancery. Officials of the chancery (*insha'*) must have fixed the proportions of the calligraphy and the precise wording to fit the decorative space. In many cases they will have had to oversee the overlapping of the inscriptions that they had composed with geometric or vegetal decoration. The prominence of calligraphy in the decorative schemes of the Alhambra meant that a dialogue between the chancery officials and the artisans was more or less inevitable. The palace's chancery seems to have played a similar role in fixing

14. A fifteenth-century silk curtain (currently in the Cleveland Museum of Art). The repetition in its design of the Nasrid motto, *La Ghalib ila Allah* ('There is no conqueror but God') makes it all but certain that it was specifically designed for the Alhambra, where the geometric and calligraphic patterns of the textiles echoed and played off the similar patterns of the stucco and tile work amidst which they were hung.

the designs as the staff of the *kitab-khanah* (library) did in Timurid Iran and Central Asia a century later. A progress report produced in 1429 and sent to Baysunqur, a Timurid prince, has survived and it gives details of the work being done in its library by calligraphers, designers, painters, bookbinders, stonecutters and workers on luxury tents. In the case of the Alhambra, it should be remembered that it was not just a matter of designing the buildings, but also the textiles and ceramics that were specifically destined for those buildings. However, though the pivotal role of the office of the *insha'* in the design of the Alhambra is most probable, it must be conceded that there is no direct evidence for this.

HEARING SECRET HARMONIES

The view that geometrical shapes and propositions express profound truths about the nature of the universe was put forward by Pythagoras (*c.* 550–500 BC). 'Justice is number 4' was one of the sayings of the disciples of Pythagoras, for they held that all abstract concepts were really expressions of number and, to take another example, ten was the number of the universe. The mathematical and ultimately harmonious nature of the universe was confirmed by experiments with a single-stringed lute. First one plucked the string to produce a note. Then one halved the string to produce a note that sounded an octave higher. Then the same string was divided in the ratio three to two and this produced a note that was a fifth higher. The ratio four to three gave a note that was a fourth higher. These things were mysteriously meant. As Keith Critchlow has put it, 'Pythagoras was the first who spoke of the nature of numbers. He taught that the nature of numbers is in relation with that of Nature. Whoever knows the nature of numbers, their species and genius and properties, can know the quantity of species of beings and their genius.' Number is 'the spiritual image resulting in the human soul from the repetition of unity'. In the centuries that followed, Pythagoreanism fed into Platonic philosophy and became indistinguishable from it. The Arabs who conquered the Near East in the seventh century became heirs to both these strands of mathematical philosophy.

In medieval Islam, mathematics was used not only for surveying and architecture, but also for such religiously related matters as the determination of the *qibla* (the direction of Mecca towards which one ought to turn to pray), the hours of the prayer times and the division of inheritances as laid out in the Koran. Mathematics had a particularly close relationship with the sister sciences of astronomy and astrology. It is also clear that pure mathematics was often a diversion for a games-playing and puzzle-solving élite. Several treatises that at first sight might seem to have been written for the use of artisans, such as the *Kitab fi ma yahtaj ilayh al-sani min al-amal al-handasiyya* ('On Those Parts of Geometry Needed by Craftsmen') by the Baghdad-based algebraist and geometer Abu al-Wafa (940–98), are now thought to have been written for the recreation of intellectuals. So that Abu al-Wafa's treatise on how to construct figures with a compass and straight edge may have been following what artisans actually did, rather than instructing them in how to do it. Given the religious applications of mathematics in the Islamic world, it is unsurprising that for most of the Middle Ages, Arab mathematics was markedly more advanced than that of the Christian West. (As late as the seventeenth century, European scholars were touring the Islamic world looking for mathematical treatises and astronomical tables that they could take home to use.) Arab mathematicians drew upon the earlier Greek work and elaborated upon it and they translated works by Euclid, Archimedes and other key figures. But they also learned a great deal from Indian mathematics and, for example, the concept of zero as well as the use of so-called Arabic numerals both derive ultimately from Indian practice.

Within the general context of medieval Islamic culture, Muslim Spain was something of a backwater. Most of the great advances in mathematical thinking were made in Baghdad, Basra and other eastern cities. However, from the ninth century onwards, the mathematical advances made in the eastern Arab lands were being absorbed by Spanish Muslim savants, and during the heyday of the Umayyad caliphate in Cordoba in the early eleventh century, Spanish Muslims, including the famous mathematician and astronomer Maslama al-Majriti (d. 1008), made important and original contributions. Even so, most advances made by the mathematicians in Spain tended to be in utilitarian areas such as the application of mathematics to land surveying and commerce and, in general, the Spaniards were better at geometry than they were in arithmetic or algebra. Moreover, though al-Majriti had disciples, mathematics went into steep decline after his death, even though there were still a few quite sophisticated mathematical thinkers to be found in Granada as late as the fourteenth century.

It was al-Majriti who was responsible for introducing an Islamic Arabic version of Pythagoreanism into Muslim Spain in the form of the *Rasa'il* ('Letters') of the Ikhwan al-Safa'

('Brethren of Purity'). The Brethren of Purity were a secretive intellectual brotherhood who probably researched and wrote in tenth- or eleventh-century Basra. Their *Rasa'il* was an encyclopedia of all the sciences with spiritual overtones, as its authors believed in salvation through mastery of the sciences. It consisted of twenty-six letters or treatises, the first of which was on number, the second on geometry and the third on astronomy. According to the Brethren, 'the science of numbers is the root of other sciences, the fount of wisdom, the starting point of all knowledge, and the origin of all concepts'. In the Brethren's Pythagorean thinking, one was the cause of all the other numbers and a good knowledge of numbers led to an understanding of God's unity. Apart from the number one, the Brethren also placed great emphasis on the number four, as 'God has created in his wisdom this universe engendered with mortality in squares (or fours) consisting of compatible and opposing (or incompatible) pairs, the secrets of which are known only to their Creator.' Geometry allowed the faculties of the soul to contemplate invisible abstract entities independently of the external world. One proceeded from tangible geometry to abstract geometry. Each geometrical figure had its own special virtue and personality.

Number, proportion and harmony structured the cosmos, so that mathematics and astronomy were inextricably linked. Four and seven governed the skies above. The Brethren envisaged the celestial vault as being divided into four parts divided by imaginary lines. Seven being the perfect number, it was inevitable that there should be seven spheres, and the human soul in its ascent to God passed through the zones of these spheres. This vision of the heavens is reproduced in the ceiling of the Hall of the Ambassadors, with its four panels and its seven ascending sets of geometrical star patterns. The 'music of the spheres' was no empty metaphor, for the Brethren believed in the literal truth of the celestial music: 'It is clear that to the movement of the spheres and of the stars there are notes and melodies … some of them touch, knock and rub one another, and resound just as brass, iron and bronze resound. And their notes are harmoniously related and their melodies are measured … like the notes of the strings of the lute.'

The music of the spheres was far more beautiful than anything that could be heard on earth. Earthly music imitates the heavenly, rather as the noises a child makes imitate those of his parents. The world was a prison from which man could free himself by religion and study and, at last, hear the heavenly music. In the mean time the enlightened listener to earthly music could be reminded of the blissful world of the musical spheres above. At a higher level yet, the music of the spheres gave those who could hear it a sense of the spiritual harmonies behind that music. Music was the subject of the fifth treatise in the Brethren's encyclopedia. It was an art that was partly spiritual and partly corporeal, which had been invented by *hukama* (sages) of ancient Greece. The *'ud* was known as the 'instrument of philosophers' and was the most perfect instrument, for its proportions matched the noble proportions of the spheres. The fact that the lute had four strings reflected an essential truth about the structure of the universe. Heptads and dodecads led the human soul to ecstasy, for twelve modes, known as *maqam*s, corresponded to the twelve signs of the zodiac, while another set of seven *azawat* corresponded to the seven spheres.

For an Arab steeped in the concepts of the Brethren of

Purity, attending a musical concert must have been a very different experience from that of a modern fan who goes to a performance of songs by Gilbert and Sullivan or by the Grateful Dead. We have already noted in an earlier chapter how a chamber like the Hall of the Ambassadors was acoustically well adapted for concerts. A Tunisian lapidarist and author, Ahmad al-Tifashi (d. 1253), wrote an encyclopedic treatise on concerts and parties, *Fasl al-khitab fi madarik al-hawass al-khams li-'uli l-albab* ('Final Say for Intelligent Minds: On the Capacities of the Five Senses'). Two chapters on music survive from this lost work. Al-Tifashi remarked on the very traditional taste in Andalusia. He concentrated on songs and music for court performances. The most accomplished singers were female and quite old and in al-Tifashi's day the best singing was to be heard in Seville.

Ibn Khaldun, Ibn al-Khatib's sometime friend and sometime rival, wrote about music, as he wrote about everything else, in his treatise on the philosophy of history, the *Muqaddima*. According to him the meaning of musical beauty 'is that existence is shared by all existent things, as the philosophers say. Therefore, existent things love to commingle with something in which they observe perfection'. Elsewhere he wrote of 'a great Sufi, who attempts to attain remoteness from sensual perception by listening to music'. Ibn Khaldun also noted how people love to sing in hot baths. Nevertheless he concluded his chapter on music with a characteristically gloomy judgement on the historical significance of singing: 'The craft of singing is the last of the crafts attained in civilization, because it constitutes the last development towards luxury with regard to no occupation in particular save that of leisure and gaiety. It is also the first to disappear from a given civilization when it disintegrates and regresses.'

The account of the Brethren's encyclopedia and their musical mysticism given here is somewhat abstract and even fanciful, but the Brethren seem to have been keen to reach out to craftsmen and convert them to their spiritual way of looking at work. Their eighth treatise was devoted to the practical arts and the techniques of artisans. Moreover, part of the treatise on geometry was actually devoted to land-measuring techniques as practised in Iraq. However, the Brethren held that contemplation of mundane things led on to the ultramundane. One of the virtues of mathematics was that its study allowed one to free oneself from attachment to the figurative (and this of course was an important consideration for a Muslim thinker).

Abstractions were peculiarly close to God, for as the Brethren put it, 'the divine works are the forms abstracted from matter and created from nothing by the Creator of everything'. Mystics as well as mathematicians studied the writings of the Brethren of Purity, and their influence on Andalusia's most famous mystic, Muhyi-al-Din ibn Arabi (1165–1240), is clear. Ibn al-Khatib and Ibn Zamrak would certainly have been aware of their doctrines.

THE PROPORTIONAL BUILDING

Recently the architectural historian and former Director of the Museum of Hispano-Muslim Art in the Alhambra, Antonio Fernández-Puertas, has argued that the men who built the two main palaces of the Alhambra 'combined an incommensurable proportional system with the use of fixed Hispano Muslim units, called *codo*s, based on the Roman *pedes*' or foot. He refers to the Arab unit as the Rashashid *codo*. (However, the Rashashid *codo* approximates to 62 or 63 cm, whereas the Roman *pes* was only 29.6 cm. I do not know why it is called Rashashid. According to my Arabic dictionary, *rashash* means 'spattered liquid' or 'dribble'.) The reason for thinking that the *codo* was the relevant unit is that this is the unit employed in a seventeenth-century *Mudéjar* manual on carpentry, *Primera y sigunda parte de las reglas de la carpintería*, by a certain López de Arenas. *Mudéjar* is the word used to refer to a Spaniard of Moorish descent, especially one who remained in Spain after 1492. The *codo* was certainly the unit of measurement employed in the eleventh-century Great Mosque of Cordoba and it has been shown to have been widely used in Muslim architecture throughout Spain.

As for the proportions, the sixth treatise in the encyclopedia of the Brethren of Purity was devoted to the moral value of proportion and the Brethren taught that beauty depended on ratios and proportions. According to Owen Jones (on whom more in the next chapter), 'Those proportions will be the most beautiful which it will be most difficult for the eye to detect.' Although there is evidence of complex geometry in most parts of the palaces of the Alhambra, the most systematic and detailed application of geometric patterning is in and round the Court of the Lions. As Fernández-Puertas notes, this was the only 'palace' to be designed by a single architect and built as a single unit within a single reign (that of Muhammad V). His exposition of the proportions of the Court of the Lions supersedes the earlier and more loosely argued theory propounded by the architectural historian Georges Marçais in the 1950s that the spacing of the arches and columns in the Court of the Lions was dictated by the golden mean, a proportional relation in which the ratio of width to length is the same as that of length to the sum of width and length. It is not clear that Muslim builders and designers ever made use of proportional relationships based on the golden mean.

Instead Fernández-Puertas argues that the grand design, as well as the detail of the court, was based on rectangles generated by square roots and surds. (A surd is an irrational number; for example, the square root of seven. The square root of seven is an irrational number in the sense that it is one that cannot be written as an integer, or whole number, or as the quotient of an integer. Pi is the most famous of the surds.) Throughout the Alhambra, builders and designers played with the ratios between irrational numbers and whole numbers. In the Court of the Lions such a ratio applied to the lengths and widths of the courtyard, as well as the heights of the columns. According to Pythagoras's theorem, a square with sides 1 unit in length must have a diagonal that is equal to the square root of 2 (=1.4142135... *ad infinitum*). If one then constructs a rectangle with a base that measures 1 unit and a side that is (approximately) equal to the square root of 2, then that rectangle will have a diagonal equivalent to the square root of 3 (=1.7320508 ...). The next rectangle generated in this fashion will have a diagonal equal in length to the square root of 4 (=2) and will evidently be a double square. Everywhere in the palaces one comes across rectangular grids that have been generated by the square roots of 2, 3, 5 etc. In addition to fixing the overall proportions of the building, the sizes of all the lesser structural and decorative elements were determined according to the same principles. For example, the decorative *lazo* of eight (eight-pointed star) was also based on the ratio of 1 to the square root of 2. The *lazo* of eight is a particularly important element in the geometric designs of the ceramic dados in the Hall of the Ambassadors. That particular *lazo* was effectively the result of rotating two squares. Much use was made of elaborations of ratios based on the square root of 2.

Incidentally, the same range of ratios seems to have been used centuries earlier in the Great Mosque of Cordoba (and, as has been noted above, the *codo* was also the unit of measurement used in the design of that mosque). Those ratios are also found elsewhere in the Islamic lands. Robert Hillenbrand has pointed out that the design of the tenth-century Tomb of the Samanids in Bukhara was based on the square root of two. In *Geometric Concepts in Islamic Art* (1976), Issam el-Said and Ayşe Parman, basing themselves on close analysis of geometrical designs from a wide range of Islamic monuments, demonstrated the role of the square root of 2 in determining the ratios of successive squares inscribed within a circle, as well as the way in which the square root of 3 was used to generate hexagonal stars. Correctly viewed, the Alhambra, like many other Islamic monuments, is as much a masterpiece of mathematics as it is of art. The mathematics is latent in the proportions of the building and its visual effect is all the more potent for its not being immediately obvious to the eye. It is not necessary to understand all of the mathematics of the Alhambra (and I am not absolutely confident that I do myself), but what must strike the eye is that, at every level, the designers of the building worked with

15. A miscellaneous selection of stone, tile and stucco fragments from various parts of the Alhambra. Girault de Prangey's *Arab and Moorish Monuments of Córdoba, Seville, and Granada, Drawn and Measured between 1832–1833* was one of the first books to popularise the details of Moorish architecture.

complexity. The complexity and detail of the design of the Alhambra defy easy reading. One is not expected to master that complexity and detail, but to drown in them. Like modern mathematicians, the medieval Arab architects were engaged in exploring infinity.

In order to understand the overall proportions of the Court of the Lions, one has first to consider the Sala de los Mocárabes on the west side of the Court of the Lions. Those who designed this area had to work within the constraints imposed by the pre-existing buildings, the Comares *hammam* to the north, a cistern to the south and the Comares Palace to the west, as well as a street to the east. These constraints determined the size of the Sala de los Mocárabes, which is five times as long (north to south) as it is wide. Next, the designer fixed the size of the courtyard by creating a rectangle generated by diagonals drawn from the corners of the eastern wall of the Sala de los Mocárabes, the inside angle of each diagonal being 60 degrees and the outside one 30 degrees. (As well as using the standard set square, *escuadro*, which produced angles of 45 degrees and 90 degrees, those who worked on the Alhambra made use of a differently shaped triangular set square, a *cartabón*, which produced the angles 90 degrees, 60 degrees and 30 degrees. An astrolabe would have been used to calculate the height of large buildings.) Similar calculations, involving diagonals and square roots, fixed the number and shapes of compartments within the Hall of the Kings, the size of pavilions on the west and east of the courtyard, the width of the surrounding galleries, the dimensions of the domed chambers on the north and south and the width of the entrance arches into those domed chambers. The calculations must have been made on the

16. The Mirador (or belvedere) of Lindaraxa, looking out over a garden. An inscription over the Mirador, composed by Ibn Zamrak, concludes, 'Surely I am in this garden an eye filled with joy and the pupil of this eye is veritably my lord'.

ground with strings and pegs fanning out from the set squares. Only in the case of the spacing of the arches on the east and west sides of the courtyard did the designer sacrifice the goal of perfect symmetry in the interest of allowing the maximum amount of light into the Sala de los Mocárabes and the Sala de los Reyes – probably the two most used rooms. A six-pointed star can be drawn on the ground plan of the Palace of the Lions in such a manner that the tips of the star touch the four corners of the courtyard, the fountain in the Hall of the Abencerrages and that in the Hall of the Two Sisters.

The size of the rhomboidal lion fountain in the centre of the patio was fixed by drawing arcs from the corners of the patio to the edges of the doorways of the two domed rooms on the north and south and having the edges of the fountain fit precisely within the intersection of those arcs. The rhomboid shape itself is based upon three rotated squares that produced a twelve-pointed star, the points of which were then joined up. The drawing of a second twelve-pointed star, created by drawing out the points of the first twelve-pointed star, seems to have fixed the location and projection of the twelve lion spouts. And so on ... The proportions of the fountain in the Court of the Lions and their harmonious relation to the rest of the courtyard indicate that the fountain was not plundered from some earlier building, but was indeed sculpted as the centrepiece for this particular layout. The vizier and poet Ibn Zamrak would have had to work very closely with the marble masons in order to produce the poem that ran along the outside of the fountain and ends with the following lines: 'And truly, is she not like a cloud who pours down her beneficence onto the lions? And in the same way, the hand of the caliph, from the first light of dawn, does he not pour his bounty upon the dogs of war?'

As in large, so in small. For example, the geometric tiles or *lazos* that are such a prominent feature of the tiled dados of the Comares Palace were designed according to rigorous geometrical principles. López de Areinas's carpentry manual gives instructions for the constructions of *lazos*. Such stars were drawn on the basis of a square grid of which the sides were 1 unit long and of which the diagonal was equal to the incommensurable square root of 2. The diagonal of the resulting *lazo* of eight was equivalent to the square root of 2. Other more complex stars were elaborated on this basic design that was so favoured in medieval Andalusia. However, it should be noted that decimal notation was unknown to medieval Andalusian mathematicians and artisans, so rather than working with the expression 1.4142135... , they relied upon approximations such as the ratio of 7 parts to 5 (7 divided by 5 does provide a tolerably close approximation to the square root of 2).

The proportional surd-based system, Fernández-Puertas believes, ultimately derived from Pythagoras, but very likely was handed down not by the scholars but rather through generations of empirically minded artisans. A silent history of craft techniques was passed on by word of mouth. Fernández-Puertas has had to work with the faintest of indications, and there is not much direct evidence for his reconstruction of how the Alhambra was designed – but then there is not much evidence for any aspect of the history of this palace. Those who have not worked as professional historians on the medieval past can have no idea of how little of that past survives, nor how many sources from which one might have reconstructed that past have vanished irretrievably.

Mathematics rather than fairy-tale whimsicality and exoticism dominated the plan of the Alhambra. Robert Hillenbrand has well observed with respect to uncritical and gushing accounts of Islamic architecture:

> It undervalues, for example, the mathematical element in Islamic architecture, and it responds to the purely visual (and excitingly alien) quality of Islamic inscriptions while remaining blind to their deliberately recondite nature, and to their role as a rebus for the faithful, as bearers of the Word and as signposts for the deeper meanings of the monuments they grace.

The Alhambra was designed according to geometrical principles. But what did all this geometry and abstraction mean to those who looked at it? Although numerous medieval Arab treatises on geometry have survived, there are no discussions of the application of geometry to aesthetic design and, for example, the word 'muqarnas' is not found in any medieval Arab dictionary, as presumably this common architectural feature did not exist in the vocabulary of the literary élite. Nor, for that matter, was there a medieval Arab word corresponding to the English 'arabesque' (see below, on this term). Although it is all but certain that Ibn al-Khatib and Ibn Zamrak were intimately involved in the design of the Alhambra, it was not the sort of thing they chose to boast about.

The employment of symmetrical tessellation is an important feature of its abstract decoration. Tessellation is the covering or tiling of an entire plane with non-overlapping shapes. Regular tessellation makes use of one shape of tile; semi-regular uses more than one. In 'wallpaper' symmetry, the pattern is repeated in all directions, up and down and sideways. In 'frieze' symmetry the pattern runs in one direction only. In 'rosette' symmetry the design motif is reflected or rotated, but without further repetition. The mathematician George Pólya has proved that there are nine basic frieze patterns and seventeen basic types of wallpaper pattern. All seventeen are to be found in Islamic art. The most obvious application of tessellation in the Alhambra is in the tile work of the various dados, where repetitive pattern is used to rest the eye. There is a kind of playfulness in this kind of pattern generation – and particularly in the way that it is often impossible to determine what is foreground and what is background. This playfulness attracted the Dutch artist who is most famous for his paradoxes, M. C. Escher. He claimed to feel an affinity for the Moors even before visiting the Alhambra. He first went there in 1926 and then again in 1936. However, though he admired Moorish tessellation techniques, he thought it a pity that they did not employ figurative imagery in their patterning. This is, of course, what Escher is famous for – making patterns based on interlocking fishes and birds, or black demons and white angels. In the course of the last century or so the study of tessellation has become an important field of mathematics in its own right, something which gives force to the following observation by the painter Tom Phillips: 'Just as art is hidden everywhere in ornament, so science also finds many of its formulations already inherent in ornamental practice. The implications of map theory, game theory, topology, the fractals of chaos theory, have all lurked in ornament, awaiting their elevation to science.' The Alhambra is a stone book in more than one sense, for not only are its walls decorated with religious and

17. A dado of tiles from a gallery of the Court of the Myrtles. This sort of
tessellation was an inspiration to the Dutch artist M.C. Escher.

poetical texts, but those texts are framed by geometrical designs that are, to all intents and purposes, demonstrations of mathematical theorems.

ARABESQUE, ATAURIQUE AND CALLIGRAPHY

'Arabesque' is an English term applied to an Islamic form of decoration that is derived from a denaturised leaf or tendril pattern and based, like the geometric star shapes, on repetition and symmetry. Some scholars with mystical or metaphysical inclinations have argued that the arabesque is a peculiarly Islamic mode of decoration and that its patterned repetition generates a sense of infinity and eternity. For example, Titus Burkhardt stated with characteristic dogmatism that 'because of its abstract nature and forms this artistic style has sometimes been referred to as "dehumanised", but in fact it gives mankind a frame to measure his own dignity; it places him at the centre whilst at the same time reminding him that he is only God's curator on earth'. However, the famous art historian Sir Ernst Gombrich has vigorously asserted the opposite. There is no evidence that the arabesque signifies Islam or infinity or any such stuff. Rather, he argues that the arabesque is one example among many in the world of visual culture of the autonomy of design. Certainly it is the case that the origins of the arabesque can be traced back to pre-Islamic, Hellenistic stylised representations of the vine leaf. It is also the case that those who have argued that it is possible to read deep mysteries in the arabesque have not been able to take their 'insight' any further. More generally Islamic vegetal or floral patterns are also designated as 'ataurique' (deriving from the

Arabic *al-tawriq*, meaning vegetation). The decorative scheme of the Alhambra relies heavily on the palmette, pine cone and palm leaf, all in stylised forms. The profusion of ataurique throughout the palaces reminds us of their interdependence with the gardens that they frame or look out upon. At times the interweaving of vegetal forms with geometric designs and calligraphic inscriptions confers a deceptive depth to the surfaces of the Alhambra.

Ataurique was often used to fill up the spaces behind or between the inscriptions. In the decorative programme carried out during the reign of Muhammad V, ataurique designs actually interlaced with inscriptions in the Kufic style. For the modern European or American visitor, the undeciphered squiggles of Arabic calligraphy add pleasing touches of decorative exoticism to the oriental palaces. But in the Middle Ages the palaces were inhabited by people who could read the squiggles. Wherever they walked or sat they were instructed by inscriptions to fear God and cringe before the magnificence of their ruler. There were boasts of Godly glory and perhaps by analogy of earthly and kingly glory too, but there were also reminders of earthly mortality and the hell-fire that awaits sinners. Those who enjoyed the pleasures of the Alhambra were reminded that those pleasures must one day come to an end. The Nasrid slogan '*La ghalib ila Allah*' ('No victor but God') was particularly pervasive. Not only was a lot of the Koran fed into the architecture, but even the poetic inscriptions that are overtly secular are suffused with Koranic references and can indeed be read as a series of glosses upon the Koran. The Alhambra, the vehicle of so many sermons in stone, is not quite the purely secular building that it appears at first sight.

18. A panel of stucco at the centre of which Kufic calligraphy is backed and surrounded by ataurique, or vegetal decoration, and is framed by geometric ornamentation. A frieze of *muqarnas* runs along the top.

Calligraphy was the only branch of medieval art where there were explicit rules and a canon of beauty. In Granada and elsewhere it was a peculiarly bureaucratic art form. The fifteenth-century Egyptian chancery official al-Qalqashandi, in his manual on chancery documents, discussed the *handasat al-khatt*, or 'geometry' of calligraphy. The scale of the letters and the ratio of the width of the strokes to their height were carefully calibrated. 'Handwriting is spiritual geometry by means of a corporeal instrument' was a saying that circulated throughout the Islamic world and was variously attributed to Plato, Euclid or Galen. So, like the geometers and architects, the calligraphers worked with an aesthetics of proportion.

Kufic was the oldest of the main styles of Arabic calligraphy and it was also one that was particularly favoured in North Africa and Muslim Spain. It was a strikingly angular script, well adapted for inscriptions on stone, and in its earliest manifestations rather austere and primitive in appearance. The form of Kufic used to adorn the walls of the Alhambra was mostly floriated Kufic in which the tops of the vertical letters break out into foliage or intertwine. Kufic was used for quotations from the Koran and these tended to be placed quite high up on the walls, whereas the poetry was usually further from heaven, and in a different style of script, known as *naskhi-thuluth*. This is a mixed script, as the pure *naskhi* style is cursive, whereas *thuluth* is more pompous and relies for its effect on the bold, broad upstrokes of the letters. The formal *thuluth* script was much favoured in the preambles of chancery documents. Usually inscriptions either ran along friezes or were set in round or rectangular cartouches.

The calligraphy of the Alhambra is readable, if with some difficulty, but what about the rest of the geometric and vegetal decoration? Could this too be 'read' by those educated Muslims who possessed the necessary skills? Why was so much effort put into interior decoration? Was the sheer quantity of decoration and repetition intended to suggest infinity? Did the geometrical designs in stucco and tile work set thought free from corporeal matters, as the Brethren had hoped? Or did the abstraction allow the viewer freedom to impose his own meaning on what he looked at? Certainly those who look around the Alhambra are not visually bossed about in the way an Italian Renaissance painting seizes the gaze and uses the linear perspectival construction, as well as the gestures and sightlines of the figures in the painting, in order to direct the eye of the person looking at the painting. Then again there is the sad possibility that Muhammad V and his statesmen paid no more attention to the decoration of the Alhambra than people do today to the wallpaper in Buckingham Palace.

In any case, not all the abstraction in the Alhambra is quite as abstract as it first appears. Attention has already been drawn to the fact that the ceiling of the Hall of the Ambassadors is a geometrically encoded representation of the seven heavens. The Koranic inscription in the hall makes that quite clear. Moreover, in considering this reference of the seven heavens and their spheres, a further level of representation may have been intended. The Brethren of Purity, in the letter on astronomy in their encyclopedia, had written of the planets as a kind of celestial court, presided over by the sun king. The moon was his chief minister and heir to the throne. Mercury was the *katib* (scribe), Mars the army commander, Jupiter the *qadi* (judge), Saturn the treasurer and Venus the maidservant. So the ordering of the planets above reflected the Nasrid court in session below.

Again consider the dome of the Hall of the Two Sisters, where the lines from the poetry of Ibn Zamrak inscribed in the hall suggest that it was metaphorically conceived of as an architectural garden under the rotating heavenly spheres. The general drift of Ibn Zamrak's poem is the boast that art has improved upon nature. The walls with their rich vegetal decoration and the floor represented a garden:

> Moreover we do not know of any other garden more
> pleasant in its freshness, more fragrant in its surroundings,
> or sweeter in the gathering of its fruits …

The ceiling represented the celestial dome above:

> The hands of the Pleiades will spend the night invoking
> God's protection in their favour and they will awaken to
> the gentle blowing of the breeze.
> In here is a cupola which by its height becomes lost from
> sight; beauty in it appears both concealed and visible.
> The constellation of Gemini extends a ready hand to help
> it and the full moon of the heavens draws near to whisper
> secretly to it.
> And the bright stars would like to establish themselves
> firmly in it rather than to continue wandering about in the
> vault of the sky …

The hall's elaborate *muqarnas* dome was built to catch and reflect the shifting light of the sun or the moon coming from the windows below and, in catching that light, mimic the movement of the stars in the sky and the rotation of the heavens. The men who built the Alhambra worked as much with light and shadow as they did with stone and wood. They used screens as filters and gilded surfaces as reflectors. It is worth noting that the alignment of the rooms and windows is usually such that the places receive more sunlight in winter than in summer. One may also consider the possible role of a mysticism of light based on certain texts in the Koran and in Sufi literature and speculate about the metaphorical role of the sultan as the sun in the cosmos of his court. At a much more down-to-earth level, the Alhambra looks very different from Versailles or Buckingham Palace and, though there are all sorts of complex cultural reasons for this, part of the explanation of why it looks the way it does is that it was built in a sunny part of the world.

IS THE ALHAMBRA PART OF THE JEWISH HERITAGE?

With the notable exceptions of the painted ceilings in the Hall of the Kings and the sculpted lions that guard the fountain in the courtyard, the Alhambra is a strikingly aniconic building. It achieves its effects through pattern and calligraphy, but, given that this is the case, there have been some striking and surprising attempts to read the buildings iconographically and to find hidden meanings in their wood and stucco. Iconography deals with the subject matter of art – the *pietà*s, banquets of centaurs, disembarkments of Cleopatra and so forth. London University's Warburg Institute, with its almost obsessive interest in the afterlife of classical Antiquity, has been preeminent in the study of iconography. It was in the *Journal of the Warburg and Courtauld Institutes* in 1956 that

Frederick Bargebuhr first published a controversial article on the meaning of the Alhambra – an article which was later expanded into a book, *The Alhambra. A Cycle of Studies on the Eleventh Century in Moorish Spain* (1968). He argued that the fourteenth-century Nasrid palace was heavily influenced by buildings put up in the 1050s by Samuel Naghralla, a Jewish vizier in the service of the Zirid ruler of Granada, on the Sabika hill on the site of the later Alcazaba, and by a magnificent palace built next door by Samuel's son and successor, Yusuf. He claimed that remains of the original sumptuous eleventh-century palace were still discernible in the foundations of the Alcazaba. The Zirid vizier is in turn presumed to have been seeking to recreate the vanished grandeurs of the Madinat al-Zahra, the old Umayyad palace outside Cordoba.

Bargebuhr suggested that not only did the fountain with its twelve lions in the centre of the Court of the Lions come from the old Jewish palace, but that this fountain was referred to in verses by the famous eleventh-century Jewish poet Ibn Gabirol:

> There is a large pool, similar to the Sea of Solomon, but it
> does not rest on bulls;
> such is the expression of the lions, at the pool's edge, that
> the cubs seem to roar through their jaws;
> and like springs, they spill their guts through their mouths,
> flowing like rivers.
> Next to the channels are sunken hollows so that water may
> be decanted to spray the plants in the garden beds with it
> and to sprinkle the stems with pure water and to water the
> garden of myrtles with it.

Following this line of thought the eleventh-century palace may have been designed to echo the opulence of the Temple of Solomon. It was possible that the twelve stone lions of the Alhambra in some sense stood in for the twelve bronze bulls that were supposed to have upheld a brazen sea in the Temple of Solomon. The general drift of the Jewish scholar Bargebuhr's argument was that the Alhambra was in a sense the belated product of eleventh-century Jewish culture, though there was also a thread of influence from pre-Islamic Persia.

All of this is exciting stuff, but it is almost certainly wrong. The word used to describe what was built on the Sabika hill in the eleventh century is '*hisn*', and that word refers to a fortress rather than a palace (which would be *qasr* or, possibly, *dar*). There is no archaeological evidence for the eleventh-century palace, as opposed to a walled enclosure. It is not clear that Ibn Gabirol's poem describes a real rather than imaginary palace. Moreover, the basin in the Court of the Lions (not a pool) is not all that large. As for the lions, Torres Balbás dated them to the fourteenth century and it seems fairly clear that they were made for the fourteenth-century fountain. Nevertheless, the thesis has been immensely influential and one finds it surfacing in numerous serious books on Islamic architecture, as well as in the guide-books. For example, Oleg Grabar in his *The Alhambra* (1978) cautiously endorsed Bargebuhr's thesis, at least in part, as well as providing additional iconographic readings of his own.

Since I have frequently cited Grabar in this book (and often approvingly), it is perhaps worth saying a little more about his approach to the Alhambra and to Islamic art in general. He has a taste for bold theorising and has been a stimulating writer and teacher. Two of his numerous books are of particular relevance to us here: *The Alhambra* and *The Mediation of Ornament* (1992). The second book seemed to take off from Grabar's reflection in one of the concluding pages of *The Alhambra* that 'as is the case with Escher's drawings and with modular contemporary architecture, a certain kind of abstraction almost compels interpretations derived from viewers rather than makers, and functions imposed by users rather than planners'. In *The Mediation of Ornament*, he surveyed the uses of geometric pattern, calligraphy and vegetal decoration, as well as figurative ornament, argued that ornament in Islamic art reached its peak in the fourteenth century and made frequent references to the decorative schemes of the Alhambra. He also discussed the theories of Owen Jones (on whom see the next chapter). At one point, Grabar quotes a medieval Jewish saying: 'A mind settled on intelligent thought is like the stucco decoration on the wall of a colonnade.' This metaphor is very much in line with the drift of his argument, which is that abstract ornamentation allows viewers to impose their own meanings upon that ornament.

That thesis seems eminently reasonable. However, in his book on the Alhambra, he took quite a different, iconographic path and suggested that the buildings once had prescribed meanings which had since been forgotten, but which can be resurrected by close reading of texts and by cross-cultural comparisons. One of his aims was to place the Alhambra in the context of Islamic palaces, while another was to demonstrate the applicability of iconography to Islamic architecture. In particular, 'complex instances of architectural iconography occur when one monument becomes a model for successive copies, imitations and transformations ...' He stressed the ghostly presence of much older buildings in the remains of the Alhambra, including Roman triumphal arches, the palace of Solomon, the throne of Chosroes, the Domus Aurea of Nero in Rome, the Umayyad palaces in both Spain and Syria and Roman rustic villas. With respect to the Court of the Lions, he further argued that it was built as a kind of victory monument to commemorate Muhammad V's capture of Algeciras in 1379 from the Christians. Well, it is possible.

The trouble is that, in the absence of much in the way of unambiguous evidence, too many theories are possible. However Grabar's book is stimulating. He is also open-minded and generous of spirit and, when the first and so far the only volume of Fernández-Puertas's massive study of the Alhambra appeared, a book which takes views that are diametrically opposed to Grabar's, the latter gave it a very fair and receptive review in the *Times Literary Supplement*. 'Volume One of *The Alhambra* is a truly extraordinary achievement' according to Grabar – a view with which I can only concur. I could not have written this book without that of Fernández-Puertas to guide me. Incidentally, Grabar's book, which has been translated into several languages, including Spanish, has been immensely influential. One of the people it influenced was Doris Lessing. The architecture of her 1980 novel (in both senses of a novel's architecture) *The Marriages between Zones Three, Four and Five* is obviously based on that of the Alhambra. In Lessing's Sufistic science fiction, architecture becomes the frame for cross-cultural interchanges and personal growth, which is perhaps what the Alhambra was intended to be in the first place.

4

THE ROMANCE OF THE MOOR

I did not take up my abode between the magic walls of the Alhambra for four days and as many nights, with the tacit consent of the authorities, neither did I dwell there for several months, attended by houris and escorted by valets descended from Moorish kings. I did not loiter about the fairy courts and halls, in the friendly silences of the moonlight, nor linger in the deep alcoves, to dream of beautiful odalisques leaning on voluptuous pillows, drowsed with the perfumes of the balmy climate and with the accents of a music sweet. While I looked down from balconies upon chivalric Granada, I did not hear a faint nocturnal sound of castanets rise from the gardens of the Darro, or the quivering pizzicato of a guitar accompany a passionate voice soaring from some solitary lane; neither did I succeed in seeing the white arm of some mysterious princess beckon from a gallery, or some dark eye sparkle through the lattice ...

Mario Praz, *Unromantic Spain* (London, 1929)

And there is more in the same vein in Praz's debunking guidebook to Spain in the early twentieth century. Mario Praz (1896–1982), a noted literary critic and academic, was a dedicated classicist and preferred the austere beauty of Palladian villas to the extravagantly decorated Alhambra. He

...orish palace to *The Thousand and One* ... was as monotonous as the other, for the ...petitive decoration seemed to him an inad- ...itute for genuine constructive power. However, ...ody quoted above was not aimed at the building so ...as at the way it and Spain more generally were written up by intellectually lazy, romantic hacks, who were so bound by cliché and possessed by the picturesque that they were blind to the realities of the land they pretended to write about. Even so, Praz's animadversions have not deterred other authors who came after him from giving the Alhambra the 'fine writing' treatment. For example, when Laurie Lee (the poet who was best known for his semi-fictitious memoir *Cider with Rosie*) wrote in his travel book *A Rose for Winter* (1955) about the wanderings of the nomadic Arabs in medieval Spain, he came up with this:

> *he found at last those phantoms of desire long sought for in mirage and wilderness – snow, water, trees and nightingales. So on these slopes he carved his palaces, shaping them like tents on slender marble poles and hanging the ceilings with decorations like icicles and the walls with mosaics as rich as Bokhara rugs. And here among the closed courts of orange trees and fountains, steeped in the languors of poetry and intrigue, he achieved for a while a short sweet heaven before the austere swords of the Catholic Kings drove him back to Africa and oblivion.*

This slack and self-indulgent way of writing about Spain's Islamic past is traceable ultimately to Washington Irving, though when Irving wrote in similar terms about the indolent and vanished joys of Moorish culture, he was at least original. Moreover, he wrote in a period when rhetorical flourish and vague generalisations about racial and cultural characteristics seem to have been demanded by the readership. Washington Irving (1783–1859), who was born in New York, made an early reputation with a collection of sketches and essays, *The Salamagundi Papers*, and a satirical *History of New York*, written under the pseudonym Diedrich Knickerbocker. Other mediocre works followed, both in the United States and England. Irving was for the most part a dull and rambling writer. He moved to England in 1815 and it was there and then in Spain that his best work was done. This included *The Sketch Book of Geoffrey Crayon, Gent*, (1819–20), which contained the famous stories of 'Rip Van Winkle' and 'The Legend of Sleepy Hollow'. Like Henry James after him, Irving was fascinated by Europe's sophistication and antiquity. In his eyes, Europe was

> rich in the accumulated treasures of age. Her very ruins told the history of times gone by, and every mouldering stone was a chronicle. I longed to wander over the scenes of renowned achievement – to tread, as it were, in the footsteps of antiquity – to loiter about the ruined castle – to meditate on the falling tower – to escape, in short, from the common-place realities of the present, and lose myself in the shadowy grandeurs of the past.

Reverence for what another writer in the Gothic vein, Horace Walpole, had called 'the true rust of the Barons' Wars' mingled with an equally familiar stock theme – that of *ubi sunt*; where now are those who came before us? Meditations on what had happened to the generations of yesteryear sat well with evocations of fallen apses, mossy walls and owls nesting in ruins.

In 1826 he moved from England to Madrid, where a post had been found for him as assistant to Alexander Everett, the US minister (consul) in the city. There were no serious duties attached to the post and he had plenty of time to research and write *The Life and Voyages of Columbus*. This biography was dull and poorly ordered, but, even before it was published in 1828, Irving was writing another book that turned out just as badly. This was *The Conquest of Granada* (1829), a work that drew heavily on the quasi-historical narrative of Gines Pérez de Hita. As a boy in New York, Irving had become fascinated with Hita's account of the civil wars of Granada, published in two volumes in 1595 and 1601, an odd mixture of history and historical novel interspersed with chivalrous ballads, which celebrated the chivalric qualities of the Moorish opponents of the Christian *Reconquista*. Above all Hita was a source for the details of the feud between the Abencerrages and the Zegries. (Irving had also read the Spanish scholar Conde on the Alhambra, before leaving America.) Boabdil, the last Muslim prince to reside in the Alhambra, occupied centre stage in Irving's rather imaginative account of the final surrender of Granada. As the troops of Ferdinand and Isabella entered the city, Boabdil and his retinue looked down from high ground on to the city they were leaving for ever:

While yet they looked, a light cloud of smoke burst forth from the citadel; and, presently, a peal of artillery, faintly heard, told that the city was taken possession of, and the throne of the Moslem kings was lost for ever. The heart of Boabdil softened by misfortunes and overcharged with grief, could no longer contain itself. 'Allah achbar! God is great!' said he; but the words of resignation died upon his lips, and he burst into a flood of tears.

His mother, the intrepid sultana Ayxa la Horra, was indignant at his weakness. 'You do well,' said she, 'to weep like a woman, for what you failed to defend like a man!'

Well, you had to be there to have known all that. (Incidentally, this is the moment alluded to in the title of Salman Rushdie's novel *The Moor's Last Sigh*.) As for the Alhambra, 'halls, lately occupied by turbaned infidels, now rustled with stately dames and Christian courtiers, who wandered with eager curiosity over this far-famed palace ...' It was more or less inevitable that Irving should think next of writing a book about Boabdil's palace and there is evidence that some of the stories that he later represented as having been told to him in the ruins of that palace had already been composed by him before he ever set foot in Granada. In Seville Irving had become friendly with the Scottish painter David Wilkie, and it may have been Wilkie who alerted him to the picturesque qualities of the Alhambra. Certainly the book that eventually appeared was dedicated to the painter.

In the spring of 1828 he went to Seville and stayed for a while with Wilkie. The following year he set off from Seville with a friend, the Russian Prince Dmitri Dolgoruki, and arrived in Granada in May. The prince did not linger long there. Irving, however, was successful in obtaining the permission of the governor of the city to lodge inside the ramshackle palace and he had as his bedroom one of the rooms that had been used by Charles V when he resided there. Irving lived in the palace from May to July. An old lady, Tía Antonia, acted as Irving's landlady, her niece was his maid and Tía Antonia's sundown *tertulia*s (gatherings) proved to be a valuable source of local lore and gossip. A young chatterbox, Mateo, acted as his guide and provided him with entertainment as well as traditional tales about the palace of ghosts, treasures and half-forgotten romances. Other picturesque characters lodged in the palaces or came visiting. In the afternoons Irving used to swim up and down the long channel of the Court of the Myrtles and claimed to have amused himself by watching urchins fly-fishing for swallows.

Irving was not the first to have alerted the English-reading world to the glories of the Alhambra. Henry Swinburne, a man of independent means who was a student of the arts and the author of *Travels Through Spain in the Years 1775 and 1776* (1779), was fascinated by Moorish architecture and wrote about the Alhambra. At around the same time the learned society Real Academia de San Fernando sent the architects Juan de Villanueva and Pedro Arnal to make drawings of the old buildings of Granada and Cordoba. The results were published in the *Antigüedades árabes de España* (1780). This book and its illustrations were in turn plagiarised by an amateur archaeologist, James Cavendish Murphy, in his *The Arabian Antiquities of Spain* (1813), a work designed to 'enable the reader to form an accurate estimate of the very high state of excellence to which the Spanish Arabs attained in The Fine Arts, while the rest of Europe was overwhelmed with ignorance and barbarism'. Murphy employed a wide variety of artists to work from his sketches and the illustrations in the *Antigüedades*. They grossly exaggerated the scale of the rooms and courtyards of the palace as well as Gothicising them. (This was a period when there was a lot of half-baked speculation about the 'Saracen' origin of pointed arches and Gothic architecture in general.) Taken as a whole, Murphy's book was a commercially inspired fantasy rather than a true record. Neither Swinburne's nor Murphy's book achieved anything like the success of that of Irving.

Swinburne had been shocked by the dilapidation of the Alhambra. Irving similarly noted that 'beautiful halls became desolate and some of them fell to ruin, the gardens were destroyed and the fountains ceased to play'. The courts were covered in graffiti, as visitors had tried to inscribe their names in history by cutting them into the wood and stucco of the palaces' walls. More ruthless visitors had taken away chunks of stucco or wood as souvenirs. (In 1828 José Contreras had barely begun work on restoration of the Alhambra.) Irving, however, saw that architectural decay could be put to literary use. *The Alhambra* was first published in 1832; he called it 'a Saracenic salamagundi'. Like several of his previous books, it is a literary scrapbook, mixing visual evocations of the place with snatches of folklore, romance, history and gossip. The narrative is as languid as the days Irving and his companions spent in the Alhambra. Irving, who described Spain as 'the land of afternoon', was obsessed with the lazy sensuality of the Moors. The decadence of the old Muslim culture had sealed the fate of medieval Granada. Like many writers who came after him, particularly Protestant ones, he contrasted past Muslim glories against a

19. This engraving of the Hall of the Abencerrages appeared in James
Cavanagh Murphy's *Arabian Antiquities of Spain* (1813–15). In keeping with
the taste of the time, Murphy grossly exaggerated the scale of the chamber,
as well as Gothicising its details.

dilapidated present and, despite the remarkably generous hospitality he had received in the Alhambra and, earlier, in Seville, he tended to present the Spaniards as lazy, ignorant, fanatical and cruel. The 'ragged and superannuated soldiers' dozing through sentry duty at the approach to the palaces were 'the successors of the Zegriés and the Abencerrages'. The noble austerity of Islam was much to be preferred to a gaudy, priest-ridden Catholicism.

> *It is impossible to contemplate this once favourite abode of Oriental manners without feeling the early associations of Arabian romance, and almost expecting to see the white arm of some mysterious princess beckoning from the balcony or some dark eye sparkling through the lattice. The abode of beauty is here, as if it had been inhabited but yesterday; but where are the Zoraydas and Lindaraxas?*

Irving used atmospheric cliché to conjure up a fantastic topography, compounded of phantoms, imprisoned princesses, buried treasures, moonlight, gypsies and *banditti*. The Alhambra was a paradise run to seed: 'The peculiar charm of this old dreamy place is its power of calling up vague reveries and picturings of the past, and thus clothing naked realities with the illusions of memory and the imagination.' There was a decidedly melancholy flavour to Irving's romanticism and he took pleasure in the ruins of the Alhambra precisely because they were ruins. He took his readers by the arm and pretended that they were actually with him as he walked about the palaces, pointing out an inscription here and a particularly fine view there. But at the same time as he used his literary arts to summon up the place in the reader's mind's eye, he was painting a self-portrait. The Washington Irving who emerges from the narrative of *The Alhambra* is mild, amiable and lazy – indeed very similar to the chief protagonist of his book, Boabdil.

'The Alhambra is an ancient fortress or castellated palace of the Moorish kings of Granada, where they held dominion over this their boasted terrestrial paradise and made their last stand for empire in Spain.' This sentence contains very nearly all the knowledge that Irving had about the history of the Nasrid palaces when he produced the first version of his book about the Alhambra. In place of dreary facts garnered from old Arabic manuscripts, Irving created a vision of the Alhambra's past that was based mostly upon legend and folklore – such stuff as the story that the red stain in the marble fountain in the Hall of Abencerrages is that of the blood of the slaughtered Abencerrages. For Irving and his generation, fables expressed the soul of the nation and were part of its history. He was a great fan of Sir Walter Scott and had visited him at Abbotsford in 1817. According to Scott, 'tradition depends upon locality. The scene of the celebrated battle, the ruins of an ancient tower, the "historic stone" over the grave of a hero, the hill and the valley inhabited by a particular tribe, remind posterity of events which are sometimes recorded in their very names.' Scott's *Minstrelsy of the Scottish Border* (1802–3) was an anthology that doubled as a kind of manifesto in favour of treating a country's legends and folklore as an important part of its historical legacy – a legacy that was in danger of being lost as traditional communities and livelihoods were menaced by social and technological change. The oral lore of humble folk was just as important as the chronicles of the knights and monks. Just as Scott often 'improved' the ballads that he rescued from oblivion, so Irving took enormous liberties with his Spanish material. Indeed the legends of the Alhambra seem to have been in large part invented or imported by him. It seems likely that some of his story motifs derive from German folklore, a field of study that Scott had got him interested in. Other elements, including the flying horse and the flying carpet, were lifted from *The Thousand and One Nights*. (Wilkie had after all requested 'something in the Haroun Al raschid style'.)

Irving's enchanted sojourn in the Alhambra was cut short at the end of July when he was summoned to take up the post of secretary at the American Legation in London. Like Boabdil, he sighed for what he was forced to renounce. 'A little further and Granada, the Vega and the Alhambra, were shut from my view and thus ended one of the pleasantest dreams of a life which the reader perhaps may think has been but too much made up of dreams.' Irving was bidding farewell to youth and irresponsibility. In London he revised his book about the Alhambra and it was eventually published in America in 1832.

Then in 1842 he was appointed American minister to Spain. His duties in Madrid do not appear to have been onerous and his second sojourn in Spain resulted in a greatly improved revised edition of *The Alhambra*, in 1851. The order was rearranged for this edition which was a third larger than the original one. In 1840 Pascual de Gayangos, the great Spanish Orientalist and a friend of Irving's, published a partial English translation of al-Maqqari's *Nafh al-Tibb*. As has already been noted, this was a chronicle which doubled as a panegyric of the life and works of Lisan al-Din ibn al-Khatib, and Irving took material from this. Later he went on to produce lots more stories and essays as well as *A Life of*

Mahomet, but never again would he write anything so good as *The Alhambra* in its revised edition. That book was influential and some of its influences are unexpected. The American showman P. T. Barnum, having read Irving, was inspired to build himself an exotic mansion in Bridgeport, Connecticut, which he called Iranistan. (It was destroyed by fire in 1857.) The tale of the Arab astrologer in Irving's book was retold in Pushkin's folk poem *The Golden Cockerel* (1835), reworked as a satire on Tsarist Russia. The Danish fairy-story writer Hans Christian Andersen carefully studied Irving's narrative technique, and the artist David Roberts was moved to visit the Alhambra after reading Irving.

THE BRITISH ALHAMBRA

The Englishman Richard Ford arrived with his family in Granada in 1831, two years after Irving. They also lodged in the Alhambra, though they do not seem to have slept so well, as Ford later complained about the rattling of the chains of the galley slaves who were working to convert part of the palace into a storehouse for salt fish. Ford published his highly successful *A Handbook for Travellers in Spain* in 1845. He affected a more hard-boiled attitude than Irving towards the Alhambra: 'Few airy castles of illusion will stand the prosaic test of reality, and nowhere less than in Spain.' The place was infested with mendicants, cripples and criminals, 'need starving in their eyes, their uniform being ragged misery. These scarecrows form fit sentinels of a building ruined by Spanish apathy.' Nevertheless Ford was also capable of using the romantic high style to conjure up the fairy palace of illusion by evening:

Then when the moon, Diana's bark of pearl, floats above it in the air like his crescent symbol, the tender beam tips the filigree arches; a depth is given to the shadows, and a misty undefined magnitude to the saloons beyond. Granada, with its busy hum, lies below us, and its lights sparkle like stars on the obscure Albaicin, as if we were looking down on the cielo bajo, or reversed firmament. The baying of a dog and the tinkling of a guitar, indicating life there, increase the fascination of the Alhambra. Then in proportion to the silence around does the fancy and the imagination become alive; the shadows of the cypresses on the walls assume the forms of the dusky moor as, dressed in his silken robes, he comes to lament over the profanation by the infidel, and the defilement by the unclean destroyer.

(No wonder Praz was exasperated.) Or consider this lament on the decay of the Alhambra: 'although her harp be unstrung, and her sword pointless, the tale of *Auld lang syne* still echoes through her bemyrtled courts'.

Ford, like Irving, peppered his guidebook with generalisations about the Spanish, most of them disparaging. In part, he was angered by their neglect of their Moorish architectural heritage: 'Familiarity has bred in them the contempt with which the Bedouin regards the ruins of Palmyra.' They called the place a 'rat's hole'. In Ford's eyes, the ruining of the place started in 1492, for the 'injuries began the very day after the conquest when the "Purifications" of the monks, that is the whitewashing and removals of Moslem symbols, commenced'. Spanish poverty and idleness went hand in hand with Romish superstition. The capture of Granada had 'paved the way to the loss of all liberty, to apathy, corruption and death'. From then on the womb of Castile was 'cursed'.

Ford was also an amateur draughtsman and a friend of the professional artist John Frederick Lewis (1805–75), who was later to become famous as a sketcher and painter of Middle Eastern scenes. Lewis had originally come to Spain to examine the works of the great Spanish masters in the Prado, before he succumbed to the lure of Moorish Andalusia. His *Sketches and Drawings of the Alhambra*, done while in Granada in 1833, contains twenty-six lithographic plates. These were somewhat impressionistic, as he did not trouble to get the decorative detail right and the detail becomes more blurred at the margins of his scenes. He later confessed to David Roberts that, when he had visited the Alhambra, he had not troubled to represent the architecture accurately. As for the monumental inscriptions in Arabic, these were depicted as a series of random squiggles. Under the Spanish sun, Lewis learned to lighten his palette, whereas previously, he had excessively favoured murky greens and browns. For Lewis, as for many painters who came after him, the Alhambra served as the gateway to the Orient and in 1837 he proceeded on to Greece and Constantinople. A little later he settled in Cairo, where he was to produce his best and most characteristic work.

Ford's sketches of the Alhambra, more accurate than those of Lewis, subsequently became the basis of the Spanish scenes by another famous artist, also a friend of Lewis's, David Roberts (1796–1864), dubbed 'the Scottish Canaletto'. Like Murphy and many other artists, Roberts seems to have thought that the Alhambra was not grand enough and his pictures improved it by exaggerating the scale. He also made the arches higher and more pointed, as the taste for the Gothic demanded. Théophile Gautier later remarked of

20. A sketch made in 1833 by John Frederick Lewis of the Comares façade, on the west side of the Court of the Cuarto Dorado. The stucco decoration of this dilapidated façade, particularly the lower part, has been reconstructed in modern times.

English artists that 'they are almost all of them out of proportion, and overloaded as they are by the necessity for rendering the infinite detail of Arab architecture, they give the
idea of a building of a much more imposing character'. Part
of the trouble was that they had all been reading Edmund
Burke's *A Philosophical Enquiry into the Origin of Our Ideas of
the Sublime and the Beautiful* (1756). 'Greatness of dimension
is a powerful source of the sublime' was one of the axioms of
Burke's influential treatise. Several of Roberts's watercolours
look like stage sets and, indeed, he had worked as a theatrical
scene painter before coming out to Spain. In 1838 Roberts
sailed for Egypt, and later visited Palestine and Lebanon,
where he worked on the sketches and watercolours that
would serve as the basis for his celebrated lithographs of
Middle Eastern landscapes. Once again the Alhambra, the
most accessible source of the exotic, had served as the
apprentice work of a great Orientalist artist.

The future Prime Minister Benjamin Disraeli was one of
the early British tourists to visit the Alhambra and he recycled his visit a couple of years later in *Contarini Fleming*
(1832), a distinctly autobiographical novel which chronicled
the roles of travel and a doomed love affair in shaping the
growth of a sensitive soul. Whether read as a novel or as a
documentary travelogue, the book is banal: 'The Spanish
women are so interesting.' Having fled 'the dull toil of vulgar
life', the narrator invites the reader to accompany him into
the Alhambra and effusively asks him to contemplate the
exquisiteness and delicacy of the decorations and indulge in
fantasies about how the place must have bustled in the time
of Boabdil. Disraeli's more substantial point was that there is
no single canon of style and the Saracenic Alhambra

21. Like Murphy before him, David Roberts was inclined to exaggerate the scale of everything in the Alhambra – as here in his portrayal of the Court of the Lions. In this early depiction of the courtyard, the eastern pavilion's roof slopes at the angle originally intended by its Moorish designers.

deserved to be ranked with the Parthenon and the Pantheon. (Chateaubriand was to make the same point.) Disraeli was an admirer of the Arabs, whom he described as 'Jews on horseback'. Moreover, he looked back with nostalgia to the centuries before the *Reconquista*, a golden age when the Jews had flourished under the tolerant rule of the Muslims.

A MEDIEVAL DESIGN MUSEUM

Irving had made Moorish architecture a backdrop for dreamy evocations of decay and indolence. However, it was also possible to use the same buildings as a pattern book for industry, moral earnestness and educational striving and this was what Owen Jones did. Jones, who was born in 1809, studied to be an artist, but he turned out to be a better draughtsman than painter. In 1833 he made a trip round the eastern Mediterranean, where he became acquainted with Islamic architecture. In Egypt he also met the Arabist Jules Goury. This was the period when scholars and artists were first becoming aware that the architecture and statuary of the ancient Greeks relied a great deal on paint and colour for their effects. Goury was already interested in Greek poly-chromy and he was fascinated by the possibilities of coloured architecture. It was natural then that he should propose to Jones that they undertake a study trip to the Alhambra.

The following year they travelled to Granada and together they set to making a visual record of the Alhambra, using a mix of plaster casts and unsized paper to record the decorative details. (Four of their plaster casts passed into the possession of the Victoria and Albert Museum.) Though Goury died of cholera in Granada in August 1834, Jones made a second visit to the Alhambra in 1837 in order to revise some of their work and make new measurements, before publishing the record of their researches. *Plans, Elevations, Sections and Details of the Alhambra* appeared in the years 1842 to 1846. This was a period when the new technology of colour printing in the form of chromolithography was just coming in and Jones's book was a pioneering work of colour printing. As such, it was very expensive. Jones, who published it himself, had to sell property to fund its publication. Richard Ford, the travel writer on Spain, was enthusiastic: 'This new style of printing in gold and colours on stone, "Lithochrysography and Lithocromatography" although the names are formidable, seems invented for this work of the Alhambra.' Jones and Goury had concentrated on recording what vestiges of paint they were able to detect on stone and stucco, though much of the once rich paintwork of the Alhambra was concealed by whitewash. However, the pictures are inaccurate in both the details of the decoration and the register of the colours. In part, this was because Jones and Goury had not been able to use scaffolding to get close to the upper parts of the walls and ceiling. In part, it was because of limitations in the capacity of chromolithography to register colours accurately. Their version of the Alhambra is a gaudy place, but the colour plates have a decidedly metallic sheen. Yet the shocking truth is that, though *Plans, Elevations, Sections and Details of the Alhambra* is incomplete and inaccurate, it is still today the most complete visual record and, if the buildings were destroyed tomorrow in an earthquake, those appointed to restore the place would be heavily dependent on Jones's publication. Moreover, Jones and Goury's pictures serve as a record of what the place looked like before speculative restoration destroyed what was originally there. And, of course, by comparison with the fantastic exaggerations and whimsical ornamentation found in images by David Roberts and others, Jones's work was downright scientific.

Jones held it as an article of faith that the increasing prominence of secondary colours was always a sign of decadence in a culture and he was doctrinaire on the dominant role of the primary colours – red, blue and yellow (or gold) – in the decoration of the Alhambra. Even so, he was obliged to note how the background of much of the stucco decoration was green, but this, he held, was because the metallic pigments had changed from blue to green over the course of time. Secondary colours were reserved for the mosaic dados, where they offered repose to the eye. He and Goury determined that there had been a tendency to use blue pigment on the surfaces that were in shade, whereas gold was painted on exposed surfaces to catch the light. Most of the columns in the Alhambra had once been gilded. Although much of the Jones–Goury reconstruction of the original colouring of the Alhambra was doctrinairely conjectural, it guided those who tried to restore the place later and, for example, the strong colours one now sees in the changing room of the *hammam* are those prescribed by Jones.

The Alhambra book was not a commercial success and it took time for its influence on Victorian crafts and design to be felt. In the mean time, Owen Jones was appointed Superintendent of Works for the Great Exhibition (1851). Henry Cole, Joseph Paxton, Owen Jones and the other key figures who worked under the patronage of Prince Albert on the Exhibition and later the Crystal Palace were earnest folk and the Great Exhibition was not intended to be a palace of fun, but rather a museum of design that would provide inspiration to the industrialists, merchants and craftsmen of the British Empire.

> All wonders of the world gladden the sight
> In that world's wonder-house the Crystal Palace;
> And everywhere is Might enslaved to Right.
>
> Martin Tupper

Joseph Paxton was responsible for erecting what looked very like a giant greenhouse in Hyde Park – the Crystal Palace. Examples of the industry and craftsmanship of the Empire and of the world were crammed within this capacious structure. As Superintendent of Works, Jones was responsible for having the framework painted in his blessed primary colours.

During the first half of the nineteenth century, it seemed to many that Britain had become the 'workshop of the world'. Its soaring industrial output led to questions being raised about the design and decoration of what was being produced. Ornament had become a matter of economic and ethical concern in a way that it had not in earlier centuries. In retrospect, what stands out was the Victorian craze for ornamental clutter and heavily patterned designs – whether in the style of Louis XIV, ancient Egypt or Moorish Spain. Gustave Flaubert was one of those who visited the Great Exhibition: 'a splendid thing, even though everyone admires it'. He took careful notes on the exotic Indian and Chinese exhibits and it is curious to reflect that the earnest pedagogic exhibition may have fuelled his later, luxuriantly orientalist fantasy, *Salammbô*. Towards the end of the year, Paxton's building was dismantled and reassembled in Sydenham, south London in 1854, where it became a permanent attraction. Within the Crystal Palace there were courts that illustrated the architecture and interior decoration of all sorts of periods and cultures – Italian Renaissance, Egyptian, Greek, Roman, Assyrian and Moorish. Jones was responsible for the last and his Alhambra Court reproduced the architecture of the Lion Court, with the Hall of Justice and the Hall of the Abencerrages crammed next to it, together with a room for plaster casts and another with divans as a Moorish-style restroom. The Crystal Palace became a popular attraction, but in the long run its pedagogic role declined and it became a centre for such popular entertainments as those then known as nigger minstrel shows.

Jones's magnum opus, *The Grammar of Ornament*, was described as 'the horn-book of angels' when it appeared in 1856, and more recently as 'a typical piece of Victorian taxonomy' by John MacKenzie. It became the most influential design manifesto of the nineteenth century. It was richly illustrated with patterns drawn from ancient Egyptian tombs, the carvings of savage tribes, Greek tombs, Mexican pottery and so on, as well as nature's own patterns of flowers and leaves. The book opened with a set of thirty-seven numbered propositions that set out the rules for 'the arrangement of form and colour, in architecture and the decorative arts'. It was the fruit of Jones's meditations on the use of ornament in other cultures and came close to being a religious treatise, since he believed that creativity was based upon religion, which was 'the teacher, the priest, the artist'. Since he viewed the Alhambra as nothing more nor less

22. Patterns of tiles copied from the walls of the Alhambra occupied an important part of Owen Jones's polemical and moralising pattern book, *The Grammar of Ornament* (1856). Medieval Moorish designs were offered to the British public as a source of inspiration to industrial and commercial design.

than 'the calm voluptuous translation of the Koran's doctrines', the decorative motifs featured in that palace were prominent in the book. The standard of perfection had been set by the Alhambra: 'Every principle which we can derive from a study of the ornamental art of any other people is not only ever present here, but was by the Moors universally and truly observed.' Jones separated the Moors from the rest of the Arabs, as he believed that the Moors were better than Arabs of Egypt, Syria and elsewhere at ornamentation and their buildings more refined and elegant. He supported the influential designer Augustus Pugin's view that decoration should grow out of architecture and, in *The Grammar of Ornament*, declared that the 'Moors ever regarded what we hold to be the first principle in architecture – *to decorate construction, never to construct decoration.*' Colour was, of course crucial: 'Form without colour is like a body without a soul.' The harmony of Moorish decoration was achieved by balancing the primary colours; where secondary and tertiary colours were used, they tended to be in the background.

According to the true gospel of ornament as laid down by Jones, illusionistic decoration was something that was almost sinful. Pattern should be abstract. For him, there was a kind of virtue in elaborate, abstract design, for 'a rich network of progressive intricacy can be seen to emerge, for it is the nature of any geometrical periodicity that it can serve to generate fresh periodicities in the hierarchy of forms'. Pattern lead the eye to move, but at the same time gave rest to the mind. According to Proposition 4: 'True beauty results from that repose which the mind feels when the eye, the intellect, and the affections are satisfied from the absence of any want.' Though Jones was a passionate exponent of the virtues of the geometrical decoration of the Alhambra, he never actually analysed it; that was left to scholars in the twentieth century. He seems to have been less interested in strictly geometrical decoration than in the arabesque. If curved lines were being employed by a designer in, for example, a pattern based on foliage or arabesque, then all lines should flow from a parent stem (as in the veins of a leaf in nature). He believed in the 'line of beauty', in which the key feature was the gradualness of the transition in a curve that breaks away from a straight line or another curve. Too abrupt a curve would be bad for the repose of the eye.

Jones's intention was not that the designs found in the tile work of the Alhambra, the tattooing of Maori faces, the brooches of the Celts and so forth should be copied. Rather their underlying logic should be understood and reapplied in new visual forms: 'The principles discoverable in the works of the past belong to us: not the results. It is taking the end for the means' (Proposition 36). *The Grammar of Ornament* with its programme of 'Design Reform' was one of the most influential books of the nineteenth century, to be ranked with Darwin's *On the Origin of Species* and Karl Marx's *Das Kapital*. In particular, Jones's attempt to set out a systematic set of rules that would explain and justify his enthusiasms was a major influence on the display and purchasing policy of the Museum of Ornamental Art (which eventually became the Victoria and Albert Museum in 1899). His ideas were also later picked up by art nouveau designers in, for example, the Saracenic designs of the jewellery of Charles Lewis Tiffany.

The architectural gospel according to Jones did not impress everybody and there were those who thought the

23. The Billiard Room at 12 Kensington Palace Gardens, London, designed in 1864 by Matthew Digby Wyatt, who 'very tastefully adapted the style of the Alhambra', most probably under the influence of his friend, Owen Jones.

decorative scheme of his beloved Alhambra was unchristian and monstrous, while Paxton denigrated his work in the Crystal Palace. Jones was rarely successful in getting architectural commissions and his theories were as often criticised as applauded. He did get commissions to build two great houses in the Moorish style in Kensington Palace Gardens, but these, like most of his buildings, have since been demolished.

DOWN WITH THE ALHAMBRA

Jones's approach to the Alhambra had been earnest and moralistic (particularly when contrasted with Irving's languorous evocations). But the famous art critic and colourful polemicist on social and economic issues John Ruskin (1819–1900) was, if anything, even more earnest and moralistic and he judged the Alhambra to be a moral obscenity. In *The Stones of Venice* and *The Bible of Amiens*, Ruskin preached the virtues of the Gothic and only the Gothic. As Kevin Jackson has remarked in *The Ruskin Alphabet*, the Gothic was, for Ruskin, 'an emotionally complex term denoting not only a style of architecture but a period of history, a Paradise Lost, an ethics of labour, a vision of order and beauty'. Ruskin was at least as pious as Jones, and his beliefs about architecture and Christianity were inextricably intertwined. The Gothic was a moral, Christian architecture. Immoral societies could not produce great art: 'You cannot paint or sing yourselves into being good men.' Rather, virtue produced great art. Ruskin believed fiercely in the work ethic and denounced useless luxury: 'see that you take the plainest you can serve yourself with – you waste or wear nothing vainly; and that you employ no man in furnishing you with any useless luxury'. So that presumably ruled out anything created by the decadent, polygamous, sensual, indolent, infidel Moors (as Ruskin imagined them to be).

The shock of the Indian Mutiny of 1857 and the reported outrages inflicted by the Indian sepoys on white women, lay behind Ruskin's loathing of Islam: 'cruelty stretched to its fiercest against the gentle and unoffending, and corruption festered to its loathsomest in the midst of the witnessing presence of a disciplined civilization, – these we could not have known to be within the practicable compass of human guilt, but for the actions of the Indian mutineer'. In *The Two Paths* (1859) he argued that ornamentation of a lower kind was the product of such cruel races as the Indians, Chinese and South Sea Islanders. Such ornamentation was like the stripes of the tiger that decorate a savage nature. In *Queen of the Air* he stated that colour sense could not be enough; moral ideas were necessary for high art and that is what the savage races lacked.

Ruskin had never actually visited the Alhambra, but he knew a lot about art and he knew what he didn't like. He formed his view of the buildings on the basis of the romantically inaccurate paintings of John Frederick Lewis. Ruskin had no trouble in discerning how horrid the Alhambra was, for its decoration was 'detestable … it is a late building, a work of the Spanish dynasty in its last decline, and its ornamentation fit only to be transferred to patterns of carpets or bindings of books, together with their marbling and mottling, and other mechanical recommendations'. The Arabs were capable only of 'doggerel ornamentation', according to Ruskin's *Modern Painters*. He returned to the attack in *The*

Stones of Venice: 'I called with deliberate expression, long ago, the decoration of the Alhambra "detestable", not merely because indicative of base conditions of moral being, but because merely as decorative work, however captivating in some respects, it is wholly wanting in the real, deep and intense qualities of ornamental art.' The Arabs, as imaginatively conjured up by Ruskin, put pleasure before the search for truth and he wrote of the Arab's fantastic spirit but exhausted genius: 'he made his architecture a glittering vacillation of undisciplined enchantment, and left the lustre of its edifices to wither like a startling dream, whose beauty we may indeed feel; whose instruction we may receive, but must smile at its inconsistency, and mourn over its evanescence'. And since Ruskin hated abstract designs, which in Britain ran in parallel with the no less detestable industrialisation and mass production, he disliked the characteristically Islamic reliance on abstraction.

In the twentieth century there were further verbal assaults on the Alhambra. In 1919 Gerald Brenan left England for Spain and settled eventually in a small remote village in the Alpujarras range to the south of Granada. As far as he was concerned, he had discovered the authentic Spain – exactly what the Alhambra was not: 'Even if that glorified gazebo, the Palace of the Alhambra, calls up during a few months of the year the boredom of dancing girls and the flicker of light and heat, the first autumn rains will quickly erase that impression.' So he wrote in his memoir *South from Granada*, and he does not seem to have liked it any better in the rain, for elsewhere he wrote: 'I saw the Alhambra in a steady drizzle, and it seemed to me shoddy and bedraggled, like a gipsy girl sitting under a damp hedge.' In 1920 Brenan's

Bloomsburyite friends, Lytton Strachey, Ralph Partridge and Dora Carrington, came out to tour southern Spain and visit Brenan. Strachey travelled with a permanently upset stomach and he took a dyspeptic view of the Alhambra, which he described as 'sheer Earl's Court'. (I have spent a long time walking round Earl's Court wondering which bits he meant, but it has since been pointed out to me that 'sheer Earl's Court' may refer to some tacky and orientalising pavilion at one of the Earl's Court Exhibitions.) Later yet, Sacheverell Sitwell, the essayist and aesthete, found the interior of the Alhambra too effeminate. The palace as a whole was boring and got more so with repeated viewings.

MASS CULTURE ALHAMBRAS

Perhaps the real problem for people with fastidious aesthetic tastes such as Strachey and Sitwell was that the place had become too popular. Tourism had given it a sheen of vulgarity. Moreover, the writings of Owen Jones had popularised the Andalusian decorative motifs and led to their being recycled in all sorts of not very appropriate buildings. As Ruskin remarked in *The Stones of Venice*, the 'Alhambra ornament has of late been largely used in shop-fronts to the no small detriment of Regent Street and Oxford Street'. And not just shops. There was even a sewage works in Stratford in East London whose interior had been inspired by the Alhambra. Even so the triumph of the Alhambra was not total. Though a few Alhambresque residences and follies were designed by Owen Jones and others, the style tended to be used for places of languor, luxury and entertainment such as smoking rooms, Turkish baths, theatres and picture palaces. The eccentric partisan of all things Turkish, David Urquhart, introduced the Turkish baths to Victorian England. Though Ottoman baths were usually rather austere in their decoration, their English counterparts tended to go for the intricate Alhambresque decoration. (An example of this kind of bath can be seen in Powell and Pressburger's fine film *The Life and Death of Colonel Blimp*.)

Of the numerous theatres that borrowed the Alhambra's name and decorative style, the grandest in Britain began its existence in 1856 as The Royal Panopticon of Science and Art in London's Leicester Square. However, when the demand for such edification proved insufficient, it was redecorated in a vaguely Moorish manner (but with Ottoman and Mameluke touches) and reopened in 1858 as the Alhambra Palace, a place for music-hall shows and other popular entertainments. Despite a bad fire in 1881, the place survived as an outpost of pastiche Islamic architecture until its demolition in 1936. From the 1920s onwards cinemas competed with live theatre and the Alhambresque was if anything even more popular with the architects of cinemas. Some of the theatres that closed their doors in the face of competition from the cinema industry subsequently reopened as cinemas, as was the case with the Alhambra Palace, which was converted into a cinema in 1929. Patrons of 'Alhambra' and 'Granada' cinemas would take their seats in stalls framed by horseshoe arches and gaze up at intricate mock *muqarnas* ceilings. Quite likely the cinema organist would favour them with a rendering of Ketèlbey's 'In a Persian Market'. The films too often showed sets based on the architecture of the Alhambra to represent the Baghdad of Haroun al-Rashid, or Ottoman Istanbul or the palace of some white sheikh deep in the

Sahara. In more recent times scenes in Harryhausen's *The Seventh Voyage of Sinbad* (1958) and his *The Golden Voyage of Sinbad* (1973) have been shot on location in the Court of the Lions and the Court of the Myrtles respectively. Bizarrely, the very specifically late-medieval Andalusian architecture has become in popular culture a kind of shorthand device for summoning up the old Baghdad of *The Arabian Nights*.

THE FRENCH HAVE AN ALHAMBRA TOO

The 'discovery' of the Alhambra had been primarily the work of Washington Irving and the British. In part, it was the evocative dilapidation of the place that appealed to these visitors (but in the course of the twentieth century that ruined charm was to be tidied away by archaeologists and administrators). In the nineteenth century Granada belatedly became a popular stopping-off point on the Grand Tour and several apprentice painters from Britain had their first encounter with the exotic in southern Spain. However, the French had their own cult of the Alhambra, which was less engaged by the details of the architecture, but more literary.

François René, vicomte de Chateaubriand (1768–1848), grew up in the sombre château of Combourg in Brittany. He fled to America in 1791 to escape the French Revolutionary Terror and described his childhood and later adventures in America in *Mémoires d'outre-tombe*. Chateaubriand was an even greater expert in romantic melancholy than Irving. In his gloom-steeped, autobiographical novel, *René* (1802), he wrote: 'I realised with a secret impulse of joy, that grief is not an emotion that one exhausts as one exhausts pleasure.' Also: 'Happiness is only to be found on the common highways' (and his aristocratic soul shrank from travelling on those). Chateaubriand needed mausoleums and ruins as backdrops for his ruminations on disappointed ambition, exile and the faded splendours of ancient faith and old nobility. A visit to the Colosseum in Rome prompted him to reflect that 'man goes to meditate on the ruin of empires; he forgets that he is himself a ruin still more unsteady, and that he will fall before these remains'. He was particularly fond of the Middle Ages, 'which offered a bizarre portrait, that seems to be the product of a powerful but uncontrolled imagination' (*Génie du christianisme*).

Over two decades before Irving's sojourn in the Alhambra, Chateaubriand visited the palace on his way back from a wilfully medievalist pilgrimage to Jerusalem, in which he had assumed the role of the last of the Crusaders. In his account of it, the *Itinéraire de Paris à Jérusalem* (1811), his visit to the Alhambra drew from him only the following banality: 'The Alhambra appeared worthy to be ranked even with the temples of Greece.' However, the romantic impact of the place also inspired (if 'inspired' is indeed the right word) him to write *Les Aventures du dernier Abencérage*. What his travelogue had kept quiet about was that Chateaubriand, who had fallen in love with the beautiful Nathalie, vicomtesse de Noailles, had undertaken the pilgrimage to prove himself worthy of her. Nathalie was painting in Cordoba and Granada and Chateaubriand had arranged to meet her in Granada on his way back from Jerusalem in 1807. Together they toured the Alhambra, followed by a deaf guitarist. Nathalie danced in the courtyards for her lover and they carved their names on a stone in the Hall of the Two Sisters. *Les Aventures du dernier Abencérage*, which commemorates in a lightly veiled fashion this romantic episode, was written shortly after this meeting, but it appeared only in 1826 because Chateaubriand delayed publication until the fall of Bonaparte and the fading of memories of France's brutal and ultimately unsuccessful campaigning in the Peninsular War. By the time he did publish his romance, the literary world of Paris had become quite bored with him reading bits out at salons.

Historically the Abencerrages, or more correctly, the Banu Sarraj, were famous for their ill fate when, during the reign of Boabdil, they were invited to a party in the Alhambra and massacred by the Zégris. However, Chateaubriand's novel was actually set in the reign of Charles V, about a quarter-century after the fall of Granada to the Christians. Its chivalric hero, Aben-Hamet, is the last surviving male member of the doomed clan of the Abencerrages, exiled in Tunis. Driven by longing to return to his ancestral home and take vengeance on those who had despoiled his ancestors of it, Aben-Hamet visits Granada in secret. Full of yearning for what has been lost to Islam for ever, he wanders through its streets. There he encounters an aristocratic young woman, Blanca, on her way to church. Blanca (who stands in for Nathalie) sings a song about the tragic fate of the Abencerrages at the hands of the Zégris. Together Aben-Hamet and Blanca visit the Alhambra, 'the home of the Genii'. It is like a palace in the old Arabian tales and its walls are like one of those oriental fabrics woven by the women of the harem. They inspect the fountain in the Palace of the Lions in which the heads of the slaughtered Abencerrages were supposed to have been placed. Aben-Hamet then reflects 'on human destiny, the vicissitudes of fortune, the fall of empires, on that of Granada itself, surprised by its enemies in the midst of pleasures: its flowery garlands suddenly turned to chains'. He also writes Blanca's name on one of the pillars, 'so that the traveller might come upon one mystery the more in this place of mysteries'. The rest of the story is about how this noble couple are united in love but separated by their respective faiths. Everybody behaves chivalrously, but it all ends sadly, as Chateaubriand seems to have believed that nobility and misery went hand in hand. It is not a very good novel, but poor stuff though *Les Aventures du dernier Abencérage* was, Chateaubriand was successful in turning the Alhambra into a shrine of romanticism for the French writers who came after him: 'Something voluptuous, something religious and something warlike seemed to breathe in this magnificent building; a kind of cloister of love, a mysterious retreat where the Moorish kings savoured every pleasure, and forgot all the duties of life.'

Chateaubriand's writings exercised a particularly strong influence on the poet Victor Hugo (1802–85). Indeed, Chateaubriand was the young poet's hero. In his early collection of poems *Les Orientales* (1829), Hugo translated Chateaubriand's penchant for the picturesque into poetry. *Les Orientales* was a flamboyantly anti-classical experiment, in which Hugo played with clichés and twisted them to produce what at the time seemed shockingly original mood-pieces that evoked sensuality and melancholy. The Greek war of liberation and the death of the poet Byron in 1824 had brought oriental matters to the fore. There was much speculation at the time about the future destinies of Islam and the Christian West. Hugo's exotic poems relied on colour and sensation rather than logical argument. In the preface to the collection, he declared that 'Spain is half African, Africa is half Asian'. Chateaubriand had called the Alhambra 'the palace of the Genii' and this epithet was taken up in one of Hugo's poems:

> L'Alhambra! L'Alhambra! palais que les Génies
> Ont doré comme un rêve et rempli d'harmonies,
> Forteresse aux créneaux festonnés et croulants,
> Où l'on entend la nuit de magiques syllabes,
> Quand la lune, à travers les mille arceaux arabes,
> Sème les murs de trèfles blancs!

'Les Djinns'

'Les Djinns' as well as another poem, 'Grenade', were loving evocations of a region that Hugo had not in fact visited. All his knowledge of Spain, Greece and the Orient came from books. In this he differed from two other figures who were chiefly responsible for familiarising the Francophone world with the glories of the Alhambra. The first of these, Girault de Prangey, was primarily an artist and his *Souvenirs de Grenade et de l'Alhambra* (1836–7), which was put together on the basis of his visits in 1832 and 1833, was primarily a picture book, in which picturesque locals posed amid the dilapidated buildings. 'Two or three convents, a few poor families living among the ruins, old invalids dying of hunger, these are the successors of the kings today.' Like Jones, de Prangey worked with the new technology of chromolithography, but though his images of the Alhambra were tolerably accurate, they were not as accurate as those of Jones. All the same, Jones owned de Prangey's book and may have learnt from it.

Just as Chateaubriand had inspired Hugo, so Chateaubriand and Hugo inspired Théophile Gautier (who later documented Hugo's impact on him in the *Histoire du romantisme*, 1872). Gautier's *Voyage en Espagne* (1841) was a lively travel book. Like many Englishmen who visited Spain in the nineteenth century, Gautier thought that the country would have fared better if it had remained Muslim. (Stanley Lane-Poole in *The Moors in Spain*, published in 1897, was to write of medieval Spain that 'for a while Christian Spain shone like the moon, with a borrowed light; then came the eclipse, and in that darkness Spain has grovelled ever since'.) Gautier moved from sleeping place to sleeping place in the Alhambra, spending four nights there. He kept his sherry cooled in the basin of the Fountain of the Lions. Though he had been fired to make the voyage by his reading of the romantics, his own prose was actually rather businesslike. Even so, he was sensitive to the melancholy ambience to which the loitering riff-raff, rubbish-strewn courtyards and general dilapidation contributed.

Having finished with the Alhambra, Gautier moved on to investigate the manner of life of the gypsies who inhabited caves in the vicinity of the Alhambra. In the decades that followed the cult of Alhambra became entwined with the cult of the gypsies of Andalusia. Gypsies were exactly what was required to dress the set of the Alhambra and highlight the sense of romantic ruin and vanished grandeur and there was a tendency to write about the gypsies as if they were in some woolly sense the heirs of the Moors. According to Gautier, their 'swarthy skin sets off the clearness of their Eastern eyes, whose fire is tempered by a sort of mysterious melancholy, the memory, as it were, of an absent fatherland and a fallen greatness'. He believed that 'at heart they have a touch of the Arab and Mahometan'. In the same year that Gautier published his travel book, George Borrow published *Zincali*, a semi-fictitious account of the time he spent with the gypsies of Spain. In the century that followed a cult of the Spanish gypsy provides much of the background to Mérimée and Bizet's *Carmen*, the music of Glinka, the paintings of Fortuny and the poetry of Lorca.

VISIONARY HAREMS AND HEADSMEN

Gautier was also a critic and partisan of 'art for art's sake' who counted several painters among his friends and protégés. Although the term 'Orientalist' (or in French '*Orientaliste*') had been used since the late eighteenth century to describe someone who studied the Orient or was enthusiastic about the region, it seems to have been Gautier who first used it to refer to a school of late nineteenth-century painters who devoted themselves to Middle Eastern and North African subjects. One of the painters he was to write about, Henri Regnault, had, like himself, visited the Alhambra and been inspired by it: 'My divine mistress, the Alhambra, beckons. She has sent forth one of her lovers, the sun, to tell me that all is ready to receive me ... Allah, you are my God, and you, Muhammad, be praised, for you have inspired such incomparable marvels. I love you because you are the father of my darling adored Alahambra ...' as Regnault wrote in a letter. Like so many artists, Regnault went to Spain to study the Spanish Old Masters in the Prado, but was then seduced by the brighter colours of Andalusia. In 1869 he visited the Alhambra in the company of another young artist who was to become a noted orientalist painter, George Clairin. Regnault was stunned by the Alhambra: 'Next to the artist who made that, we are barbarians, savages, monsters.' Having made numerous sketches and notes, he moved on to Morocco in a continuing quest for the relics of medieval Moorish culture.

In Tangiers, Regnault drew upon his notes to paint his most famous canvas, *Summary Execution under the Moorish Kings of Granada*. The painting (now in the Musée d'Orsay) shows an enormous Moorish headsman wiping his bloody sword as he looks down on his just-decapitated victim. The ornately decorated and golden glowing architecture, that seems to owe something to the Cuarto Dorado and something to the belvedere of the Lindaraxa, provides a spectacular backdrop to the savage scene. Though the subject matter is exotic, its representation is naturalistic. Indeed, like many orientalist painters, Regnault worked from photographs. By the 1860s there was already a tourist trade in photographs of the Alhambra. He described his painting as showing 'the richest civilisation and the keenest cruelty coexisting in titanic, frightful splendour'. He envisaged his broader programme as an artist as being 'to depict the real Moors in the way they used to be, rich and great, both terrifying and voluptuous, the ones that are to be found only in past history'. Regnault's career was dazzling but short. In 1870 he returned to France to volunteer for the Franco-Prussian War and was killed in the fighting.

In recent decades *Summary Execution* has been denounced as 'orientalist' in a pejorative sense. Regnault has been condemned for conjuring up a barbarous Orient in order to supply a Western audience with a dubious *frisson*. However,

24. Henri Regnault's brilliant but shocking version of *Summary Execution under the Moorish Kings of Granada* (1869) juxtaposes exotic architecture, violence, delicacy and power. Though the decorative repertoire of the Alhambra has been used as a backdrop to the execution, the painter has produced a composite version of the Alhambresque, rather than an accurate reproduction of any particular room.

when one considers the abrupt and sanguinary way in which Nasrid sultans and viziers dealt with one another, one cannot claim that Regnault's painting represents a libel on the Alhambra's past. We live in an age when it is commonplace to denounce the painting of executions and tortures, while implicitly exonerating the acts themselves. Orientalist painting is no longer fashionable – except, that is, with rich Arab collectors, most of whom live in the Gulf region. In the nineteenth century contacts between literary and visual artists were much closer than they are these days and nineteenth-century painting was a thoroughly literary affair. A great deal of the orientalist painter Gérôme's current renown (if that is the word) is due to attacks on him by anti-orientalist polemicists such as Rana Kabbani, Edward Said and Linda Nochlin. Jean-Léon Gérôme (1824–94) specialised in paintings with literary and historical themes, many of them set in the Orient and featuring odalisques, harem guards and snake charmers. This sort of subject-matter is now linked with a latently imperialist agenda and is widely held to be unacceptable. There have also been sneers at his licked-finish style. (Like Regnault, Gérôme liked to work from photos.) Gérôme went to Spain in 1873 and later used a free version of the Court of the Lions in the Alhambra as the background to two renderings of the same theme – *The Grief of the Pasha*. In both paintings the carcass of the tiger is spread out on a carpet in the court and the pasha sits on one corner of the carpet and broods with his head resting on his hand. It is a painted version of a poem in Hugo's *Les Orientales*, 'La Douleur du Pacha', the closing verse of which runs as follows:

Non, non, ce ne sont pas ces figures funèbres,

Qui, d'un rayon sanglant luisant dans les ténèbres,
En passant dans son âme ont laissé le remord.
Qu'a-t-il donc ce pacha, que la guerre réclame,
Et qui, triste et rêveur, pleure comme une femme? …
Son tigre de Nubie est mort.

(But of course there are no tigers in Nubia. Nor pashas. Besides, one of the candlesticks seems to come from Mameluke Egypt, whereas the carpet, whatever it may be, is certainly neither Spanish nor medieval. It looks as though it was manufactured in a factory in Brussels.) Hostile discussions of Gérôme's work have focused on the minority of paintings that show slave girls or dilapidated buildings (signals of oriental corruption and decay), but paintings such as *The Grief of the Pasha* or *The Chess Players* escape criticism or even mention by those who hate Gérôme.

There is no space here to discuss the hundreds of orientalist paintings by Hercules Brabazon, Filippo Baratti, Mariano Fortuny. Regnault's lurid rendering of a Moorish execution notwithstanding, in general the painters conjured up visions of the old Moorish way of life in the Alhambra that were favourable, even idealised. Artists who painted the Alhambra, or Egyptian carpet bazaars or Turks at prayer did so in response to a public demand (channelled through the commercial galleries of Paris and London) for paintings of subjects that allowed a kind of escape from contemporary urban and industrial life, poverty, mass markets, social unrest and grey skies. John Mackenzie, a historian specialising in the British Empire, has queried the tightness of the links made by Said, Nochlin and others between the exoticism of orientalist painting and imperialism and racism:

Indeed, when other imperial art is considered, it is apparent that Orientalism celebrates cultural proximity, historical parallelism and religious familiarity rather than true 'Otherness'. It is surely for this reason that several artists initially sought out the East in Europe. David Roberts and J. F. Lewis, Georges Clairin (1843–1919) and Henri Regnault (1843–71) among others, visited Granada and portrayed the architecture and culture of Moorish Spain before they ventured further afield.

It was not always necessary for the French even to travel as far as Spain to experience the glories of the Alhambra that Chateaubriand, Gautier, Regnault and others had celebrated. Just as the Crystal Palace had its Lion Court, so too a Lion Court was erected for the Paris Exposition of 1900. The big theme of the exhibition was old Paris, but there were also reconstructions of an Algerian and an Indo-Chinese village, as well as a vast exhibition devoted to the theme of 'Andalusia in the Time of the Moors', that sprawled over the Trocadéro Gardens. Surviving photographs suggest that the reconstruction of the Lion Court was only approximate. However, in order to give a greater feeling of authenticity, North Africans in native dress were paraded through the court. This *belle époque* celebration of Moorish culture, 'incontestably the most brilliant epoch in the history of Spain', was implicitly also a derogation of the Spanish Catholic culture that had replaced it.

SPAIN, THE MIDDLE EAST IN THE WEST?

According to the Romantic poet Alfred de Vigny, a 'Spaniard is an Oriental, he is a Catholic Turk, his blood

25. In the Caliph's palace in old Baghdad the evil wizard Sokurah, in order to
entertain Prince Sinbad and his bride-to-be, has transformed a servant
woman into a four-armed, snaky dancer. Actually much of Harryhausen's
immensely enjoyable *The Seventh Voyage of Sinbad* (1958) was filmed in the
Alhambra. Besides featuring the Court of the Myrtles complex (as here), the
film also set scenes in front of the Partal and even the Palace of Charles V.
The Alhambra again stood in for Baghdad in Harryhausen's *The Golden
Voyage of Sinbad* (1974).

either languishes or boils, he is a slave to indolence, ardour, cruelty ...' The alleged contrast of the contemporary, ignorant, decadent, lazy, Papist Spaniard with his cultured Moorish predecessor was extremely popular with other European and American writers. So it is not surprising that many Spaniards looked on the Muslim heritage in Andalusia with ambivalence and even hostility. It was common for Spaniards in the nineteenth and twentieth centuries to argue that it was precisely Arab barbarism which had held Spain back from becoming a fully modern European nation. There was also a tendency to reattribute Arab cultural artefacts to Christians, as nothing really good could possibly have been done by infidels.

Some of Spain's leading thinkers lined themselves up firmly on the side of the medieval Catholic *Reconquista*. The thinker, poet and novelist Miguel de Unanumo (1864–1936) was one of them: 'About the Arabs I have nothing to say; I have a profound dislike for them, I hardly believe in what is called Arab civilization and I consider their passage through Spain to have been one of the greatest misfortunes we have ever suffered' (*El porvenir de España*, Madrid, 1912). José Ortega y Gasset (1883–1955) was another, and he argued vigorously against the idea that modern Spain owed anything to its Moorish past. The nineteenth-century historian of medieval Granada Francisco Simonet drew on Ibn Khaldun's argument in the *Muqaddima* that the 'Arabs' ruined every land they passed through. (However, Simonet chose to ignore the fact that in this context Ibn Khaldun was referring only to nomadic Arabs.) Even in more recent times, hostility to Moorish culture has persisted in some circles in Spain. The Arabist Emilio García Gómez (1905–95) did important work on the Alhambra and became head of the school of Arab studies that was set up in Granada in 1932. Despite his intense familiarity with Moorish culture, he was not really very fond of it. He considered that the poverty of the materials used in the Alhambra was an indicator of the decadence of Nasrid culture, 'corroded by internal viruses, the slave of an irremediable past'. In 1943 he produced *Ibn Zamrak, el-poeta de la Alhambra*, a study of literary and court life in the fourteenth-century Alhambra that placed heavy stress on the decadence of that environment. Another Arabist, A. R. Nykl, wondered why García Gómez had chosen to study a subject he did not seem to like very much.

On the other hand there was a long-standing, countervailing disposition among the 'afrancesados', or 'Frenchified' Spaniards who were enlightened supporters of democracy and liberal and secular principles. There was a tendency among the liberal intelligentsia to take pride in the Moorish past and deplore the persecution of Muslims and Jews instituted by the Catholic authorities after 1492. Josef Antonio Conde (1766–1820), one of Irving's sources on the history of Moorish Spain, was an early representative of these 'afrancesados'. So was the gentleman-dilettante Don Pascual de Gayangos y Arce (1809–97) who translated part of Maqqari's life of Ibn al-Khatib into English in the 1840s. One of the reasons why he published an English translation was that he had gone into exile in London. He later also wrote the highly literary introduction to Jones and Goury's book on the Alhambra. Partisans for Moorish culture and the glories of the Alhambra tended also to be partisans for the Republic when it was set up and sided with it in the Spanish Civil War. The medievalist Americo Castro, who liked to stress the

Arab and Jewish role in forming Spanish culture and who declared modern Spain to have been born in 711 (the year the first Arab and Berber armies crossed the Straits of Gibraltar into Spain), ended up as an exile from the Franco regime. Influenced by contemporary events, the distinguished Orientalist Angel González Palencia (1889–1949) went so far as to argue that the *Reconquista* was really a civil war between the followers of the two faiths. As the Israeli historian of medieval Islam David Wasserstein has written,

> *Spaniards have, until very recently, tended to view the Islamic element in the history of the peninsula in terms of the general debate about the nature of Iberian, Spanish identity. Even when they have not rejected the Muslims and all their works outright, even when they have gone far over towards the opposite extreme, their arguments over identity have made their writings on the broader history of Islam in Spain an integral part of the debate itself, and in doing so have led often to attempts to present that Islamic history in ways which suit present political and social Iberian needs.*

The same ambivalence and questioning of cultural identity is to be found among Spanish artists, writers and musicians. The cases of the musician Manuel de Falla and the poet Federico García Lorca are instructive. The two were friends and both knew García Gómez. However, they took a rather different approach to Moorish culture. Falla (1876–1946) mocked Debussy, the composer of the *Puerto del Vino* prelude and *Les Soirées de Grenade*, for never having set foot in Granada and for having composed his music on the basis of postcards that Falla had shown him. But Falla's knowledge of and enthusiasm for medieval Granada was not so great either. At the time Falla composed *La Vida Breve*, he had never set foot in Andalusia and he had to write to friends asking for postcards of Granada. Throughout his career he himself faced accusations that his music was too influenced by the French. García Gómez remarked of Falla that he 'abhorred the Arab poison and, after his own country, he loved the best that the Latin Occident has produced: Rome with its eternal stones, and Provence with its courts of love and Venice of Tintoretto, the Tuscany of Dante and the Paris of Debussy.' Lorca (1899–1936), on the other hand, grew up in Granada and as a young man embraced a kind of cult of the Alhambra and made frequent trips up the hill to the palaces. He even used to dress as a Moor. Later, his enthusiasm for Islamic culture cooled somewhat and Andalusian gypsies replaced Moors as a source of inspiration. In his poetry he created a stylised fantasy world populated by passionate and violent gypsies. However, towards the end of his brief life, he met García Gómez and studied the translations of Andalusian Arab poetry that the scholar had started to publish in 1930. In 1936, year of the outbreak of the Spanish Civil War, Lorca gave a radio talk about how he regarded the contrast between the Nasrid palaces and that of Charles V as emblematic of the divide in contemporary Grenadine society. There was also a furore when Lorca described the fall of Muslim Granada as a disastrous event. Fascists murdered him later that year.

THE ARAB ARCADIA

In modern times the Alhambra raised troubling questions

about the cultural identity of the Spaniards. For Arabs and Muslims, on the other hand, the monument has come to stand for all that they have lost in recent centuries – not just in Spain, but also territories in the Balkans, India and elsewhere, as well as the end of the caliphate, the eclipse of Arab science and philosophy and a decline of cultural confidence. The Alhambra serves as an icon of exile and loss. In *Tales of the Alhambra*, Washington Irving related how one day he had encountered a turbaned Moor from Tetuan in the Court of Lions. They walked about the palace and as the Moor made out the inscriptions on the walls, he lamented the vanishing of the power and the glory of the Muslim sovereigns of the place. Irving reported that there were families in North African cities who 'retain the ancient maps and deeds of the estates and gardens of their ancestors at Granada and even the keys of the houses, holding them as evidences of their hereditary claims, to be produced at the anticipated day of restoration'. I suspect that this encounter was invented and that a fictitious Moor served Irving as a peg for yet more reflections on the vanished glories of the Moorish past, as well as serving as an introduction to his apologetic account of the unhappy reign of Boabdil. Nevertheless, from the nineteenth century onwards, the Alhambra did indeed become a place of pilgrimage for Arabs who mourned the vanished glories of Islam and the caliphate and even today there are Muslims who pray for the restoration of Granada to Muslim rule. (Some of them have settled in Albaicín, just across the Rio Darro from the Alhambra, where they have been joined by Sufis, as well as Arabs dealing in leatherwork, ceramics, hookahs and mint tea.) When Disraeli was making his Grand Tour in 1830 his travelling companion, William

Meredith, 'noted that the old lady who showed them over this splendid edifice was quite convinced that "Benjamin D. was a Moor, many of whom came to visit this palace which, they say, will be theirs yet again." His southern aspect, the style in which he paced the gorgeous apartments and sat himself in the seat of the Abencerrages quite deceived her.'

In the course of the nineteenth century, a considerable cult centred on the lost civilisation of Andalusia grew in the Muslim world, even though some more rigorous Muslims who visited the Alhambra were disturbed by the secular and sensuous feel of the buildings and the occasional appearance in them of figurative imagery, including the painted kings on the ceiling of the Hall of the Kings and the sculpted lions in the courtyard. The cult of the sunset glories of Andalusia was fuelled by growing Muslim familiarity with Western orientalist writings that celebrated the civilisation of Cordoba and Granada and the past achievements of the medieval Arabs more generally. Lane-Poole's *The Moors of Spain* (1897) and Gustave le Bon's *La Civilisation Arabe* (1884) exercised a particularly strong influence on Muslim thinkers and writers. Le Bon's was a work of higher vulgarisation, written by an unscholarly hack who knew no Arabic, but his book was popular because of the extravagant claims it made for the Arabs and their influence on European culture. He claimed that until the fifteenth century it was hard to find any medieval European author whose work consisted of anything more than copying the Arabs. (His book was translated into Arabic as *Hadrat al-Arab* in 1969.)

Some leading Arab authors had a more direct knowledge of Moorish civilisation. The Egyptian neo-classical poet Ahmad Shawqi (1868–1932) was fervently pro-Ottoman and during the First World War, at the behest of the British, was sent into exile in Spain. Shawqi eschewed modernist innovation and wrote poems in the manner of the famous eleventh-century Andalusian poet Ibn Zaydun. Even before his exile to Spain, he had evoked that land in a poem written in 1912 in which he lamented the Muslims' loss of Macedonia in that year:

> Farewell, sister of Andalusia,
> Islam and the Caliphate have fallen from thee
> The crescent moon has gone down from thy sky.
> Would that the heavens had folded up
> And darkness enveloped all the globe.

In another poem, 'An Andalusian Exile', Shawqi made an implicit comparison between his own plight and those driven from Spain by the *Reconquista*. The famous Syrian intellectual Kurd 'Ali visited Granada in 1922. He arrived on 27 January, when the anniversary of the fall of the city to the army of Ferdinand and Isabella was being celebrated. Church bells rang and there was feasting, but, in Kurd 'Ali's eyes, the people he walked among were celebrating a historical tragedy – a triumph of ignorance over science – and he gloomily speculated that Morocco (which was then a French colony) would be the next place from which the Arabs would be expelled. The Syrian poet Nizar Qabbani (1923–98) was also a diplomat, one of whose official postings was to Madrid. Though chiefly famous for his love poetry, he also wrote poems on political themes in which he occasionally dwelt on the lost land of the Arabs in Spain. In Qabbani's poetry the historical tragedies of the Arabs were inextricably mingled

[183]

with his own personal tragedies. His son was kidnapped and killed and his wife was blown up in an explosion at the Iraqi embassy in Beirut. He ended up in exile in London. For another poet, the Palestinian Mahmud Darwish, what happened in Spain foreshadowed the disasters of modern times: 'Andalus became a lost place, then Palestine became Andalus; we lost Palestine just as we had lost Andalus.'

In the Arab consciousness, the Alhambra is populated by ghosts and is the object of backward glances and heavy sighs. Recently the well-known Lebanese novelist and member of the Arab literary diaspora Hanan al-Shaykh produced an essay entitled 'In the Court of the Lions I Sat Down and Wept'. She did not weep because the Arabs were no longer in charge of Granada, but because

> we Arabs today have no connection with the Arabs of Andalusia, with those who, having borrowed the pens and chisels of angels, have carved and embellished to such melodious perfection …
>
> Why is it that we didn't complete our cultural journey, and how is it that we have ended up today in the very worst of times? What is it that made our predecessors pore over their desks, writing down and recording the marvels of mathematics and science and searching out the skies with the stars and constellations in order to discover their secrets, and, driven by the love of knowledge, to study medicine and to devise medicaments even from the stomach of bees. It is enough for us to mention the works of al-Farabi, Avicenna, Ibn Khaldun, Ibn Rushd, Ziryab, Ibn Hazm, Ibn Zeydoun and countless others.

Hanan al-Shaykh reports a religious sheikh who was faced with this sort of question and 'scratched his beard with assured confidence. "It doesn't matter," he said. "This world is for them and the Hereafter is for us."' But Hanan al-Shaykh is rightly contemptuous of such dismal apologetics.

It is curious that such a beautiful place should be pervaded by such melancholy associations. Jorge Luis Borges visited the Alhambra in 1976 and wrote a poem on the last days of Boabdil:

> Your gentle ways now depart,
> your keys will be denied you,
> the faithless cross will wipe out the moon,
> and the evening you gaze upon
> will be the last.

MAKING A VISIT?

You are advised to visit the Alhambra out of season, as the queues in the summer trail a long way down the hill. The flow of tourists is controlled by timed tickets, which can be pre-booked by telephone or on the internet. The Patronato of the Alhambra estimates that the passage of no more than 350 people per hour through the buildings is manageable. At the time of writing, typing 'Alhambra' on Google produces approximately 402,000 hits. However, the Patronato have their website at the head of the list and this provides full details of opening times, prices and so forth.

Having visited the Alhambra by day, you must also visit it by night to get a full sense of how the place was inhabited. It is also important to sit on the ground often in order to view the place as it was intended to be viewed. The Museum of the Alhambra in the Palace of Charles V should on no account be missed as substantial chunks of the old palaces have ended up there. These include marble capitals, tombstones, the wooden door of the Hall of the Two Sisters, a fountain from the Lindaraxa garden, a Nasrid throne, tiles with figurative imagery from the Peinador, a magnificent Alhambra jar, and much else. The presence of other objects from elsewhere in Muslim Spain also makes it possible to trace the evolution of Nasrid art from its Umayyad and Almohad antecedents. Apart from the Alhambra itself, most of what has survived in Granada from Moorish times is located in Albaicín across the valley – definitely worth exploring.

Not all of the Alhambra has stayed in Granada. The Museo Arqueológico Nacional in Madrid possesses various items, including a lamp from the vanished mosque. Berlin's Museum für Islamische Kunst has the original ceiling from the Torre de las Damas of the Partal Palace. In the United States, the Cleveland Museum of Art and the Cooper-Hewitt Museum in New York both possess silk hangings which look as though they were made for the Alhambra. Alhambra vases have ended up in museums in Palermo and St Petersburg, as well as in the Museum of the Alhambra.

There is nothing from the Alhambra in the (soon to be revamped) Islamic Gallery in London's Victoria and Albert Museum. However, the museum is planning to stage a smallish display in the new Architecture Galleries devoted to the Alhambra. This will include stucco and tile fragments from the Alhambra, an inscription and a marble column, as well as scale models. If all goes to plan this will open in autumn 2004. The V&A also possesses some of the plaster casts made by Jones and Goury, but these, it seems, will not be going on display. In the British Museum's John Addis Gallery (for Islamic art) there is a ceramic border with calligraphy from the Peinador de la Reina. In the recently opened Enlightenment Gallery there are four pieces of tile from the Hall of the Ambassadors, which bear the calligraphic coat of arms of the Nasrids and which were acquired by Anne Seymour Damer (1749–1802), a protégée of Horace Walpole and a sculptor, who had visited the Alhambra after reading Henry Swinburne's *Travels through Spain*. She gave the tiles to the British Museum in 1802.

FURTHER READING

THE ALHAMBRA

The fundamental book on the history of the Alhambra is undoubtedly Antonio Fernández-Puertas's *The Alhambra, I, From the Ninth Century to Yusuf I (1354)* (London, 1997). However, it is large, expensive and unfinished. (There are two further volumes scheduled.) Though this work was originally commissioned as a text to accompany reproductions of the plates of Owen Jones and Jules Goury, it is far more than that. It is a painstaking history of the Alhambra up to but not including the reign of Muhammad V and its close analysis of the complex decorative schemes and architectural layout of the Alhambra makes for rewarding, though rather hard reading. The footnotes are often lively, as Fernández-Puertas is keen to correct the errors of his predecessors. It also points out some of the mistakes made by Owen Jones in his attempt to make a visual record of the Alhambra. Important reviews of this book appeared by Oleg Grabar in the *Times Literary Supplement* (7 November 1997), pp. 12–13 and by Michael Rogers in the *Bulletin of the School of Oriental and African Studies*, 61 (1998), pp. 335–6. Fernández-Puertas produced an intensely condensed account of his views on the Alhambra for the *Macmillan Dictionary of Art* (under 'Granada'). Also well worth consulting is Fernández-Puertas, 'The Three Great Sultans of al-Dawla al-Isma'iliyya al-Nasiriyya who Built the Fourteenth-Century Alhambra: Isma'il I, Yusuf I, Muhammad V (713–793/1314–1391)', *Journal of the Royal Asiatic Society* (1997), pp. 1–25. This provides a concise account of the political and cultural context of the building of the Alhambra.

On the palace of Charles V the definitive work is by Earl E. Rosenthal, *The Palace of Charles V in Granada* (Princeton, 1985). See also Cammy Brothers, 'The Renaissance Reception of the Alhambra: The Letters of Andrea Navagiero and the Palace of Charles V', *Muqarnas*, 11 (1994), pp. 79–102. Sanford Shepard, 'Islamic Monuments in Christian Hands', *Islamic Culture*, 46 (1972), pp. 293–5 is a brief highly critical account of the fate of the Alhambra after 1492. Otherwise, most of the scholarly work on the Alhambra has been published in Spanish and to a lesser extent in French. *The Alhambra* (London, 1978) by Oleg Grabar has been discussed in Chapter 3. It is well written, stimulating and makes fascinating comparisons between the Alhambra and other Islamic palaces (what little we know of them). However, some of its hypotheses about the iconography of the Alhambra are almost certainly wrong. In part, Grabar relied too much on F. Bargebuhr, *The Alhambra: a Cycle of Studies on the Eleventh Century in Moorish Spain* (Berlin, 1968). Though the publication of Bargebuhr's book was an important event in the history of Alhambra studies, its conclusions are now widely disputed. See in particular the review of Bargebuhr by Rachel Arié in *Der Islam*, 52 (1975). Grabar's book was rather fiercely reviewed by James Dickie,

'The Alhambra: Some Reflections Prompted by a Recent Study by Oleg Grabar', in Waddad al-Qadi (ed.), *Studia Islamica et Arabica: Festschrift for Ihsan 'Abbas* (Beirut, 1981), pp. 127–49. However, some of Dickie's own theses seem unduly dogmatic. Grabar, *The Mediation of Ornament* (Princeton, 1992) is a difficult though rewarding study of the types of decoration employed in various cultures. Though it ranges widely, both the Alhambra and Owen Jones loom large. Ernst Gombrich, *The Sense of Order* (second edition, Oxford, 1984) covers similar ground and is similarly stimulating. Tom Phillips's profoundly interesting ideas on ornament appear as 'Summary Treatise on the Nature of Ornament', in *The Architectural Review* (April 2003), pp. 79–85. Keith Critchlow, *Islamic Patterns: An Analytical and Cosmological Approach* (London, 1976) provides a useful summary of Pythagorean ideas. Issam El-Said and Ayşe Parman, *Geometric Concepts in Islamic Art* (London, 1976) graphically demonstrates how surds lie behind much of Islamic geometrical pattern-making.

Michael Jacobs, *Alhambra* (London, 2000) looks like a coffee-table book, as it is a large-format work with colour plates, but the text is intelligently argumentative and draws on the author's wide knowledge of Spanish culture. (He has also written on Barcelona, Andalusia, the pilgrimage to Compostela and Lorca.) However, Jacobs is not an Arabist and the book's strength is really in dealing with the afterlife of the Alhambra under the Christians. Among more specialised works, Jerrilynn Dodds, 'The Paintings in the Sala de Justicia: Iconography and Iconology', *Art Bulletin*, 61 (1979), pp. 186–95 is the most recent and substantial study of those mysterious paintings. The case for the Court of the Lions having been originally paved in marble was put by Enrique Nuere Matauco, in 'Sobre el pavimento del Patio de los Leones' (in *Cuadernos de la Alhambra*, 22 (1986), pp. 87–93. The case for regarding the Court of the Lions as a *madrasa* is presented by Juan Carlos Ruiz Souza in '*El Palacio de los Leones de la Alhambra: ? Madrasa, zawiya y tumba de Muhammad V? Estudio para un debate*, published in *Al-Qantara*, 22 (2001), pp. 77–120. James Dickie, 'Towards an Aesthetic of Grenadine Art', *Oriental Art*, new series 26 (1980) pp. 323–31 is stimulating, even if, in my case, I am sometimes stimulated to disagree. *Arte islámica en Granada. Propuesta para un Museo de la Alhambra* (1995) is an exhibition catalogue that effectively doubles as the catalogue of the Museum of the Alhambra (inside the Palace of Charles V). Many of the objects illustrated come from the Alhambra, including examples of woodwork, ceramic, stucco, tombstones, furnishings and fabrics.

Then there is J. Augustin Núñez (ed.), *The Alhambra and Generalife in Focus* (Madrid, 1991). This is the book to have in one's hands as one walks about the Alhambra. It is compact, lavishly illustrated, beautifully designed and tolerably up to date in its conclusions. It draws on the expertise of a range of Spanish scholars and besides taking the visitor step by step through the buildings and gardens, it has useful inset sections on such matters as the ceramics, lighting and flora of the Alhambra. Published by Edilux in Spain, it does not seem to be available in Britain, but several shops within the grounds of the Alhambra sell it. There are plenty of competing guidebooks, but buy this one. Also available in the shops of the Alhambra is a CD-Rom, *La Alhambra: Realizado con Vistas Inmersivas de 360˚*. This disc, which comes with text options in Spanish, English and German, affords the viewer the illusion of walking through the various rooms of the palaces and being able to look around and up and down, as well as to examine chosen areas more closely. It is a fine souvenir or, more seriously, a useful *aide-mémoire* of your visit.

THE HISTORY AND LITERARY CULTURE OF MOORISH SPAIN

There is not a vast amount in print in English about the history of Muslim Spain. Richard Fletcher, *Moorish Spain* (London, 1992) is a readable, short book mostly on the political history of al-Andalus, though it also deals with cultural matters. Fletcher's book is noteworthy for its disinclination to exaggerate the extent of Muslim cultural achievements or its toleration of other faiths (though, to be sure, both were considerable). The standard work on the political history is Hugh Kennedy, *Muslim Spain and Portugal: A Political History of al-Andalus* (London, 1996). This is a much more detailed narrative than Fletcher, and, unlike the latter, who was dependent on translations, Kennedy draws directly on Arabic source materials. However, he does not discuss the art or literature of Muslim Spain. The standard and authoritative work on the history of Nasrid Granada is Rachel Arié, *L'Espagne musulmane au temps des Nasrides (1232–1492)* (second edition, Paris, 1990). This lengthy, detailed work not only provides a (rather dry) narrative history of the Nasrids, but has chapters on the topographic background, political institutions, the army, judiciary, society, economy, private life, literature and the arts. As far as the history of the Alhambra is concerned, Arié seems to be in full agreement with the views of Fernández-Puertas.

Salma Khadra Jayyusi (ed.), *The Legacy of Muslim Spain* (London, 1994) is a great book, over 1,100 pages long, and contains many valuable essays that are relevant to the Alhambra, including Robert Hillenbrand on Cordoba, Oleg Grabar on Andalusian art, Jerrilynn Dodds on Andalusian architecture, Fernández-Puertas on Andalusian calligraphy, and James Dickie on Granadan urbanism, on space and volume in Andalusian architecture, as well as on gardens. María Rosa Menocal et al. (eds.), *The Cambridge History of Arabic Literature: The Literature of Al-Andalus* (Cambridge, 2000), despite its title, does not confine itself to literature and includes Dodds on spaces, D. F. Ruggles on the Great Mosque of Cordoba and Alexander Knysh on that key figure, Ibn al-Khatib. My own *Night and Horses and the Desert: an Anthology of Classical Arabic Literature* (Harmondsworth, 1999) includes brief accounts of and excerpts from Ibn Zamrak, Ibn Khaldun and Ibn al-Khatib, as well as Ibn al-Khatib's biographer, al-Maqqari. The key ode on the Alhambra by Ibn Zamrak is discussed by Akiko Motoyoshi, 'Poetry and Portraiture: A Double Portrait in an Arab Panegyric by Ibn Zamrak', *Journal of Arabic Literature*, 30 (1999), pp. 199–239. Ibn al-Khatib is also the subject of a short monograph in Spanish, Emilio Molina López, *Ibn al-Jatib* (Granada, 2001).

ANDALUSIAN AND ISLAMIC ART AND ARCHITECTURE IN GENERAL

Jerrilynn Dodds (ed.), *Al-Andalus, the Arts of Islamic Spain*

(New York, 1992) is the lavishly illustrated and learned catalogue of the Metropolitan Museum's exhibition of Andalusian art. It includes three chapters on the Alhambra, as well as an important article by D. Fairchild Ruggles on the Alhambra's gardens and Islamic gardens in general. Marianne Barrucand and Achim Bednorz, *Moorish Architecture in Andalusia* (Cologne, 1992) is very well illustrated. Godfrey Goodwin, *Islamic Spain* (London, 1990 and now out of print) was a Penguin paperback for the guidance of tourists on the tracks of Islamic architecture in Spain.

Robert Hillenbrand, *Islamic Architecture: Form, Function and Meaning* (Edinburgh, 1994) is a stylishly written and challenging book that takes a typological approach to palaces, mosques, minarets, *madrasa*s, mausolea and caravanserais. However, the eloquent evocation of the Alhambra that I have quoted in Chapter 1 comes from Hillenbrand's *Islamic Art and Architecture* (London, 1999). In *La madrasa médiévale* (Aix-en-Provence, 1995) Lucien Golvin provides an account of the architecture of Muslim teaching colleges. Sheila S. Blair and Jonathan M. Bloom, *The Art and Architecture of Islam* (Yale, 1994) can also be unreservedly recommended. Apart from its learned text, it also has beautiful and well-chosen pictures. Of particular interest is its last chapter, 'The Legacies of Islamic Art', which discusses the impact of Islamic art on such figures as Owen Jones. Doris Behrens-Abouseif, *Beauty in Arabic Culture* (Princeton, 1999) provides a pioneering discussion of what we can deduce about Arab aesthetics up to 1500. Michael Rogers discusses the architectural economies of the fourteenth-century Egyptian sultans in 'The Stones of Barquq', *Apollo* (April 1976), pp. 307–13. Lisa Golombek, 'The Draped Universe of

Islam' in Priscilla P. Soucek (ed.), *Content and Context of the Visual Arts in the Islamic World* (London, 1988), pp. 25–50 is a wide-ranging discussion of the importance of textiles in Islamic art and architecture. My own *Islamic Art* (London, 1997) is one of several competing general introductions to Islamic art. What distinguishes mine from the others is, first, its non-chronological approach; secondly, an unusually heavy reliance on textual sources to shed light on the artefacts; thirdly, the emphasis the book places on the problematic nature of what we think we know about Islamic art.

With respect to the calligraphy of the Alhambra, the findings of Fernández-Puertas (published both in his book on the Alhambra and in Jayussi's *The Legacy of Muslim Spain*) are crucial. On Islamic calligraphy more generally, a good starting point is provided by Annemarie Schimmel, *Calligraphy and Islamic Culture* (New York, 1984).

On other Islamic palaces, see Robert Hamilton's brilliant study of the eighth-century Umayyad palace of Prince Walid in the Jordan valley, *Walid and His Friends: An Umayyad Tragedy* (Oxford, 1988). Grabar has suggestive remarks about Abbasid and other palaces in his *The Formation of Islamic Art* (New Haven and London, 1973). Also the relevant chapter in Hillenbrand's *Islamic Architecture*.

GARDENS

Gabrielle van Zuylen, *Alhambra, A Moorish Paradise* (in the 'Small Books on Great Gardens' series, London, 1999) is a pretty little picture book. For more substantial accounts of Muslim and Andalusian gardens, see in particular D. Fairchild Ruggles, *Gardens, Landscape, and Vision in the*

Palaces of Islamic Spain (University Park, Pennsylvania, 2000). Also, Richard Ettinghausen (ed.), *The Islamic Garden* (Washington DC, 1976), Jonas Learman, *Earthly Paradise: Garden and Courtyard in Islam* (London, 1980) and James Dickie, 'The Hispano-Arab Garden. Its Philosophy and Function', *Bulletin of the School of Oriental and African Studies*, 31 (1968), pp. 237–48. *A Moorish Calendar from the Book of Agriculture of Ibn al-Awam* (Wantage, 1979), translated by Philip Lord, is a late twelfth-century agricultural manual written by an Arab living in the Guadalquivir.

ISLAMIC THOUGHT AND CULTURE

On medieval Arab mathematics, see Juan Vernet, 'Mathematics, Astronomy, Optics' in Joseph Schacht and C. E. Bosworth (eds), *The Legacy of Islam* (Oxford, 1974), pp. 461–88; George Gheverghese Joseph, *The Crest of the Peacock: Non-European Roots of Mathematics* (London, 1991). On the Brethren of Purity, see Seyyed Hossein Nasr, *An Introduction to Islamic Cosmological Doctrines: Conceptions of Nature and Methods Used for Its Study by the Ikhwan al-Safa', al-Biruni and Ibn Sina* (Cambridge, Mass., 1964), Ian Richard Netton, *Muslim Neoplatonists: An Introduction to the Thought of the Brethren of Purity* (London, 1982). Ibn Khaldun's *magnum opus* on the underlying principles of history has been translated by Franz Rosenthal as *The Muqaddimah: An Introduction to History*, 3 vols (second edition, London, 1967). The life and work of Ibn Khaldun have attracted a large secondary literature – just how large is suggested by the bibliography of over 850 items listed in Aziz al-Azmeh, *Ibn Khaldun in Modern Scholarship: A Study in Orientalism* (London, 1981).

The arguments and insights presented in Jonathan Bloom's *Paper Before Print: The History and Impact of Paper in the Islamic World* (New Haven and London, 2002) have crucial implications for the history of Islamic art and literature. The quotations from the Koran are taken from A. J. Arberry, *The Koran Interpreted* (London, 1955 and reprinted many times since).

THE AFTERLIFE OF THE ALHAMBRA

Washington Irving's *The Alhambra*, first published in 1832, has frequently been reprinted since. It is on sale in most of the shops within the enclosure of the Alhambra and throughout Granada. The most widely available edition includes pleasing though romantically inaccurate engravings from the romantic period. There is a two-volume biography of Irving: Stanley T. Williams, *The Life of Washington Irving* (New York, 1935). See also Marwan M. Obeidat, 'Washington Irving and Muslim Spain', *International Journal of Islamic and Arabic Studies*, 4 (1987), pp. 27–44. Théophile Gautier's *Voyage en Espagne* (Paris, 1845) was translated by Catherine Alison Phillips in 1926 and reprinted in 2001 as *A Romantic in Spain*. Chateaubriand's *Les Aventures du dernier Abencérage* was translated into English in the nineteenth century, though frankly it is not worth reading in any language. Owen Jones's *The Grammar of Ornament*, first published in 1856, has been reprinted several times, most recently as a large format paperback by L'Aventurine in Paris in 2001. Ruskin returned to the hideousness of the Alhambra and of Islamic art in general again and again – in *The Two Paths*, *Modern Painters* and *The Stones of Venice*. Michael Snodin and

Maurice Howard, *Ornament: A Social History Since 1450* (London, 1996) puts the ideas of Owen Jones, Ruskin and others in a broader context.

Early encounters with the Alhambra are the main topic of Tonia Raquejo, 'The "Arab Cathedrals". Moorish architecture as seen by British Travellers', *Burlington Magazine*, 128 (1986), pp. 555–64. Raleigh Trevelyan, *Shades of the Alhambra* (London, 1984) is a lively general book, which mainly focuses on the impact of the place upon such figures as Washington Irving, Chateaubriand and Manuel de Falla. David Mitchell, *Travellers in Spain* (London, 1990) cites the responses of Richard Ford, Lytton Strachey and others to the Alhambra. For the influence of the Alhambra and other Islamic buildings on European architecture, see John Sweetman, *The Oriental Obsession: Islamic Inspiration in British and American Art and Architecture 1500–1920* (Cambridge, 1988), Miles Danby, *The Islamic Perspective* (London, 1983), Danby, *Moorish Style* (London 1995); John M. Mackenzie, *Orientalism: History, Theory and the Arts* (Manchester, 1995). The chapter in Mackenzie's book on orientalist painting is also well worth reading. Walter B. Denny, 'Quotations in and out of Context: Ottoman Turkish Art and European Orientalist Painting', in *Muqarnas*, vol. 10 (1993), *Essays in Honor of Oleg Grabar*, pp. 219–30 has some sharp observations about Gérôme, albeit only in a Turkish context. A much more negative view of Orientalist painting is taken by Linda Nochlin in 'The Imaginary Orient' in that author's volume of essays, *The Politics of Vision: Essays on Nineteenth-Century Art and Society* (Boulder, Colorado, 1989). The recreation of the Lion Court in Paris in 1900 is discussed in Roger Benjamin, *Orientalist Aesthetics: Art Colonialism and North Africa*

1880–1930 (Berkeley and Los Angeles, 2003). There is plenty to read about David Roberts, including Helen Guiterman, *David Roberts, R.A.*, (London, 1981) and Katharine Sim, *David Roberts R.A.: A Biography* (London, 1984). Helen Guiterman and Briony Llewellyn, *David Roberts* (London, 1986) is an exhibition catalogue with useful essays. On Lorca, see Ian Gibson, *The Death of Lorca* (London, 1973) and Leslie Stainton, *Lorca. A Dream of Life* (London, 1998). On Falla, see J. B. Trend, *A Picture of Modern Spain. Men and Music* (London, 1921) and Jaime Pahissa, *Manuel de Falla* (London, 1954). James T. Monroe, *Islam and the Arabs in Spanish Scholarship (Sixteenth Century to the Present* (Leiden, 1970) deals with the frequently acrimonious debates within the academic community about the extent of the debt owed by modern Spain to its Moorish past. Gerald Brenan's animadversions on the Alhambra were published in *South from Granada* (London, 1957). Philip Guedella's beautifully judged historical fantasy 'If the Moors in Spain Had Won …' was published in J. C. Squire (ed.), *If It Had Happened Otherwise* (London, 1932, reprinted 1972). Hanan al-Shaykh's essay 'In the Court of the Lions I Sat down and Wept' was published in English and Arabic in the American magazine *Gobshite* in winter 2003. Dick Davis's poem 'The City of Orange Trees' appears in *Devices and Desires. New and Selected Poems 1967–1987* (London, 1989).

LIST OF ILLUSTRATIONS

While every effort has been made to contact copyright-holders of illustrations, the author and publishers would be grateful for information about any illustrations where they have been unable to trace them, and would be glad to make amendments in further editions.

ACKNOWLEDGEMENTS

I would like to acknowledge the assistance of the following in putting this book together: Helen Irwin, Mary Beard, Peter Carson, Robert Hillenbrand, Fiona Buckee, Dick Davis, Hugh Kennedy, Maribel Fierro, Venetia Porter and Hanan al-Shaykh. I suppose that it is vain to hope that any mistakes I make will be blamed on them.

INDEX

WONDERS OF THE WORLD

This is a small series of books that will focus on some of the world's most famous sites or monuments. Their names will be familiar to almost everyone: they have achieved iconic stature and are loaded with a fair amount of mythological baggage. These monuments have been the subject of many books over the centuries, but our aim, through the skill and stature of the writers, is to get something much more enlightening, stimulating, even controversial, than straightforward histories or guides. The series is under the general editorship of Mary Beard. Other titles in the series are:

Published
Mary Beard: **The Parthenon**
Richard Jenkyns: **Westminster Abbey**
Simon Goldhill: **The Temple of Jerusalem**

Unpublished
Cathy Gere: **The Tomb of Agamemnon**
Keith Hopkins and Mary Beard: **The Colosseum**
John Ray: **The Pyramids and the Sphinx**